Sentence Composing
10

HAYDEN WRITING SERIES

ROBERT W. BOYNTON, *Consulting Editor*

Sentence Composing
10

DON KILLGALLON

Baltimore County Schools

HAYDEN BOOK COMPANY, INC.
Rochelle Park, New Jersey

Library of Congress Cataloging in Publication Data

Killgallon, Don.
  Sentence composing 10.

  (Hayden writing series)
  Includes bibliographical references.
  SUMMARY: A textbook focusing on the composition
of sentences by using four sentence-manipulating techniques:
scrambling, imitating, combining, and expanding.
    1. English language—Sentences—Juvenile literature.
1. English language—Sentences. I. Title. II. Series.
PE1441.K47   808'.042   79-26479
ISBN 0-8104-6122-6

Copyright © 1980 by HAYDEN BOOK COMPANY, INC. All rights reserved.
No part of this book may be reprinted, or reproduced, or utilized in any
form or by any electronic, mechanical, or other means, now known or
hereafter invented, including photocopying and recording, or in any information storage and retrieval system, without permission in writing from
the Publisher.

Printed in the United States of America

3   4   5   6   7   8   9   PRINTING

82 83 84 85 86 87 88   YEAR

To Jenny
for coaching, cheering, and often carrying the ball.

Preface

This series—SENTENCE COMPOSING *10, 11,* and *12*—emphasizes the most neglected unit of written composition: the sentence. Using four sentence-manipulating techniques—*sentence scrambling, sentence imitating, sentence combining,* and *sentence expanding*—the books teach students structures they seldom use in their writing, but should and can easily use once they become familiar with them through many examples and Practices.

Each book concentrates on such structures by means of model sentences by professional writers. The rationale is based on the widely accepted mimetic theory of *oral* language acquisition, applied here to *written* language acquisition in the belief that continual exposure to structures used often by professionals in their sentences will produce attention to, understanding of, and, with practice, normal use of such structures by students in their sentences.

The books are exercises in applied grammar, with the theory and terminology of grammar subordinate to the major goal, composing sentences. The naming of parts and the parsing of sentences, the goals of traditional grammar study, are exercises in dissection. The practices in *Sentence Composing* are exercises in production.

The sentence-manipulating techniques are easily learned. The Practices based on them are interesting and challenging, and they can be done by any student. In addition, the teacher can readily give attention to the sentences students compose, with quicker, more constant, and more thorough feedback than with longer compositions.

Since the Practices have proved successful for the great majority of students who have used them in pilot programs in all kinds of schools, it is demonstrably true that *Sentence Composing* can work anywhere—in any school, with any student.

DON KILLGALLON

Baltimore, Maryland

Contents

Sentence Composing
10

Introduction: How Sentence Composing Works

When you write sentences and when professional writers write sentences, you both engage in a similar process. The results, however, are often different, sometimes dramatically so. The difference isn't spelling, capitalization, or other conventions of written English. It's true that many students have problems with such matters. It is also true that you rarely find mechanical flaws in published writing. Authors are not necessarily better in these respects; they may just have good editors.

A big difference (and the one this textbook deals with) is in sentence structure variety. You will recognize this difference as you practice "sentence composing"—that is, producing sentences closely resembling in structure those written by professional writers. *Sentence Composing 10* focuses on sentence structure as a major difference between the sentences of professionals and those of students. The text provides model sentences written by professionals. You will practice writing your own sentences with structures similar to the ones in the models. The goal is to establish those structures in your own writing.

PRACTICE

Although it's important for you to become aware of differences in sentence structures, you don't have to know a lot about grammar to describe such differences, as you will see in the Practice below. The structures in the sentence pairs are different: one is like a professional writer's; the other is not. Can you tell which is which? What is the difference? (The answers are in the References.)

1a.   That was Tom's great secret, the scheme to return home with his brother pirates and attend their own funerals.

b.   Tom had a secret, which was to return home with his brother pirates and attend their own funerals.

Based on a sentence by Mark Twain, The Adventures of Tom Sawyer

2a.   Her eyes looked like two small pieces of coal and were lost in the fatty ridges of her face, and they pressed into a lump of dough as they moved from one face to another while the visitors stated their errand.

b.   Her eyes, lost in the fatty ridges of her face, looked like two small pieces of coal pressed into a lump of dough as they moved from one face to another while the visitors stated their errand.

Based on a sentence by William Faulkner, "A Rose for Emily"

3a.   I seemed forever condemned, ringed by walls.

b.   I seemed forever condemned because walls ringed me.

Based on a sentence by Richard Wright, *Black Boy*

4a.   It was a heavy, hard, sharp, and not rolling sound.

b.   It was a heavy sound, hard and sharp, not rolling.

Based on a sentence by Theodore Taylor, "The Cay"

5a.   Its pelvic bones crushed aside trees and bushes while it ran, and its taloned feet clawed damp earth to leave prints six inches deep wherever it settled its weight.

b.   It ran, its pelvic bones crushing aside trees and bushes, its taloned feet clawing damp earth, leaving prints six inches deep wherever it settled its weight.

Based on a sentence by Ray Bradbury, "A Sound of Thunder"

6a.   She was only thirty feet from one sleek, plump dolphin when she shot into the air, landed with a crash in the water, and lay there motionless, shaking her head in an almost human manner.

b.   She was only thirty feet from one sleek, plump dolphin, then she shot into the air and landed with a crash in the water, and she lay there motionless and then shook her head in an almost human manner.

Based on a sentence by Arthur C. Clarke, *Dolphin Island*

7a.   There was no water except at the time of the spring rains, and very little desert vegetation.

b.   There was no water except at the time of the spring rains, and desert vegetation was also scarce.

Based on a sentence by Naomi Hintze, "The Lost Gold of the Superstitions"

The section called References contains the original sentences by professional writers. These sentences were the bases for most of the Practices in this book. They are included so you will have immediate feedback on how you did in the individual Practices. They should not be considered "answers in the back of the book." They are for comparing your sentences with the professionals' sentences. The important thing is not whether your sentences duplicate the professionals', but whether you learn anything from the comparison. You may decide that a particular professional sentence is better; in that case, study the differences. You may decide that yours is just as good; in that case, congratulate yourself. You may decide that yours is better; in that case, take a bow. In any case, the important thing is that the References are not "answers."

In this book you will study four sentence composing techniques that will enable you to write sentences similar in structure to those of professional writers: sentence scrambling, sentence imitating, sentence combining, and sentence expanding. In addition, you will learn how to apply these techniques in the writing of paragraphs: paragraph expanding. The techniques themselves are easy to learn; however, in order to apply them to your own writing, you must practice them frequently. The book provides numerous practices for that reason. Don't make the mistake of thinking that just because you can do the technique, you will apply it in your own writing. The application of the skill to your own writing is more likely to occur if you do most of the practices on the particular sentence composing technique emphasized in each section of the book.

You can learn much about writing in general, not only sentence structure, through the practices in this book. The study of the sentence has too often been neglected as a way of improving writing; instead the study of the sentence was used mainly for analyzing grammar. *Sentence Composing 10* studies the sentence as a way of improving your writing. Even though you will be working mostly with sentences, there is much that you can learn about good writing of any length and type—paragraphs, essays, short stories, reports, and research papers.

1
Sentence Scrambling

DEFINING SENTENCE SCRAMBLING

Sentence scrambling simply means mixing up the parts of a sentence and then putting them back together to make a meaningful, well-written sentence. Sentence scrambling permits a close look at how professional writers assemble the parts of their sentences.

    The sentence parts are printed as a list in a different order from that in the original sentence. To illustrate, here is an original sentence, a list with the sentence parts in the same order as in the original, and a list with the sentence parts scrambled.

Original Sentence

When his father, who was old and twisted with toil, made over to him the ownership of the farm and seemed content to creep away to a corner and wait for death, he shrugged his shoulders and dismissed the old man from his mind.

Sherwood Anderson, Winesburg, Ohio

Original Order

1. When his father,
2. who was old
3. and twisted with toil,
4. made over to him the ownership
5. of the farm
6. and seemed content
7. to creep away
8. to a corner

9. and wait for death,
10. he shrugged his shoulders
11. and dismissed the old man
12. from his mind.

Scrambled Order

1. to a corner
2. from his mind.
3. and wait for death,
4. When his father,
5. he shrugged his shoulders
6. made over to him the ownership
7. who was old
8. and dismissed the old man
9. of the farm
10. and twisted with toil
11. to creep away
12. and seemed content

The sentence parts in sentence scrambling are all grammatical units that make up the structure of the sentence. Each sentence part has meaning. Only when all the parts are joined together, however, is there sentence meaning. To recognize sentence parts that are not grammatical units, try to make sense out of the word groupings in this list:

1. When his
2. father, who was
3. old and twisted with
4. toil, made over to
5. him the ownership of
6. the farm and seemed
7. content to creep away to
8. a corner and
9. wait for death, he
10. shrugged his
11. shoulders and dismissed the old
12. man from his mind.

Because none is a grammatical unit, none by itself makes sense. Because all of the sentence parts in the previous list were grammatical units, each one by itself makes sense.

We read and write in meaningful "chunks." We mentally identify "chunks" as a series of words that are meaningful in contributing to our understanding of the rest of the sentence. The "chunks" are meaningful in two ways: in content and in grammar. Each "chunk" may be considered a sentence part that has its own content and its own grammar.

Let's look at an example. We'll use this sentence, a condemnation of the evils of tobacco written in 1604 by James I:

[Tobacco is] a custom loathsome to the eye, hateful to the nose, harmful to the brain, dangerous to the lungs, and in the black, stinking fume thereof, nearest resembling the horrible Stygian smoke of the pit that is bottomless.

"A Counterblast to Tobacco"

Below are two versions of the sentence with slash marks. In one, the slash marks are placed at random with no attempt to indicate where "chunks" of meaning might be. In the other, the slashes indicate meaningful divisions or "chunks" in the sentence. To find out which has the meaningful "chunks," try reading both. The one easier to read is the one in which the slashes indicate meaningful "chunks." The other version will be difficult to read, like any hodgepodge of unrelated groups of words. (Punctuation has been omitted.)

A.   Tobacco is a/custom loathsome to/the eye hateful to the nose harmful/to the brain dangerous/to the lungs and in the/black stinking fume thereof nearest/resembling the horrible/Stygian smoke of/the pit that is/bottomless.

B.   Tobacco is a custom/loathsome to the eye/hateful to the nose/harmful to the brain/dangerous to the lungs/and in the black stinking fume thereof/nearest resembling/the horrible Stygian smoke/of the pit/that is bottomless.

We read and write in meaningful "chunks," not in meaningless groups of words. Writing, like reading, is the process of communication of parts of a whole message, done in an orderly, logical fashion, one "chunk" at a time, sentence part by sentence part.

PRACTICE 1

To make sure you understand how we read (a "chunk" at a time) and, more importantly for *sentence composing,* how we write sentences (sentence part by sentence part), try the following exercise. See if you can discriminate between the version divided into meaningful "chunks" and the version divided into meaningless groups of words. Read according to the slash lines, letting your eye span take in only those words from one slash mark to the next. It might help to read the sentences aloud. If it appears that you are reading gobbledygook, that version is the meaningless one; if reading is easy, that is the one divided into relatively meaningful "chunks." Punctuation has been omitted. When you have identified the meaningful sentence, decide how you would punctuate it.

1a. I am not/ashamed to confess that/I am/ignorant of what I/do not know.

b. I am not ashamed/to confess/that I am ignorant/of what I do not know.

Cicero

2a. If you/put a chain around the/neck of a/slave the other/end fastens/itself around your own.

b. If you put a chain/around the neck/of a slave/the other end/fastens itself/around your own.

Ralph Waldo Emerson, "Compensation"

3a. If a man bites/a dog that/is news.

b. If a man/bites a dog/that is news.

John Bogart

4a. A pessimist/is one who feels bad/when he feels good/for fear he'll feel worse/when he feels better.

b. A pessimist is one who feels/bad when he/feels good for/fear he'll feel/worse when he feels better.

Anonymous

5a. Optimism is a/cheerful frame of/mind that enables a tea/kettle to sing though/in hot water up/to its nose.

b. Optimism is/a cheerful frame of mind/that enables a tea kettle/to sing/though in hot water/up to its nose.

Anonymous

6a. There are three marks/of a superior man/being virtuous/he is free from anxiety/being wise/he is free from perplexity/being brave/he is free from fear.

b. There are three marks of a superior man being/virtuous he is free/from anxiety being wise/he is free from perplexity being brave/he is free from fear.

Confucius

7a. To have and to hold from this day forward for better/or for worse for richer/or for poorer in sickness/and in health to love/and to cherish till death/do us part.

b. To have and to hold/from this day forward/for better or for worse/for richer or for poorer/in sickness and in health/to love and to cherish/till death do us part.

Book of Common Prayer

The writer of sentences composes in this one-step-at-a-time fashion—or should; otherwise, the result is a jumble, clear perhaps in the mind of the writer and easy to get down on paper, but confusing and uncomfortable to read. Be wary of too easy writing. Someone once said, "Easy writing is hard reading." Keep in mind the reverse of this statement: "Hard writing is easy reading."

PRACTICE 2

To reinforce your understanding of meaningful sentence parts, do this activity. Copy each sentence below twice. Insert three slash marks into each sentence in each pair. The first time, place the slash marks in places representing meaningless divisions. The second time, place them to represent meaningful divisions. (See the previous Practice for examples.) Finally, punctuate the sentence.

1.   A politician thinks of the next election a statesman of the next generation.

James Freeman Clarke

2.   A politician is an animal who can sit on a fence and yet keep both ears to the ground.

Anonymous

3.   It is of great importance in a republic not only to guard against the oppression of its rulers but to guard one part of society against the injustice of the other part.

Alexander Hamilton

4.   In a free country there is much clamor with little suffering in a despotic state there is little complaint with much grievance.

Lazare Carnot

5.   Those who deny freedom to others deserve it not for themselves and under a just God cannot long retain it.

Abraham Lincoln

6.   I would rather sit on a pumpkin and have it all to myself than to be crowded on a velvet cushion.

Henry David Thoreau

7.   If you would not be forgotten as soon as you are dead either write things worth reading or do things worth writing.

Benjamin Franklin

PRACTICING SENTENCE SCRAMBLING

Read the four short sentences below:

1.   Ralph bit a dog.

2.   A vase bit a necklace.

3. A bit dog Ralph.

4. A dog bit Ralph.

The sentences illustrate two kinds of meaning: content meaning and grammatical meaning. Which two have content meaning that makes sense, even though one is a little far-fetched? Which one has content meaning that is nonsense?

In the next Practice you will be using an important characteristic of language: grammatical meaning. All of the above four sentences—except one—have grammatical meaning. Which one does not have grammatical meaning?

If a sentence has grammatical meaning, we will be able to "read" it. The next Practice uses nonsense content to allow you to focus only on the structure of sentences (grammatical meaning) rather than on the specific content of sentences.

PRACTICE 3

In these two lists of scrambled sentence parts, the content is nonsense, but the structure is grammatically meaningful. The sentence parts are scrambled versions of the model sentence above the lists. Unscramble them to produce a sentence identical in structure to the model.

Model

When his father, who was old and twisted with toil, made over to him the ownership of the farm and seemed content to creep away to a corner and wait for death, he shrugged his shoulders and dismissed the old man from his mind.

Sherwood Anderson, Winesburg, Ohio

List One: Nonsense Sentence Parts (In Scrambled Order)

1. and covered the floor
2. and feathered with grease
3. with its typewriters
4. which was solid
5. when the ashtray
6. sang for him the dance
7. and became encouraged
8. to an ocean
9. the crab blanked its pencil
10. and hope for mud
11. of the petunia
12. to jump up

List Two: Nonsense Sentence Parts (In Scrambled Order)

1. in an instant
2. which was crystal
3. the bun opened its halves
4. although the hamburger
5. ran down to him the story
6. in a dictionary
7. of the onion
8. and demented in town
9. and seemed reluctant
10. and study for words
11. to fly away
12. and embraced the cheese

PRACTICE 4

Match, then list, the equivalent sentence parts in all three sentences—the two imitations and the model of Practice 3.

PRACTICE 5

This activity will help you become aware of differences in sentence structures. Below are four sentences, each different from the next, not only in content but in sentence structure. All four are between twenty and thirty words long. Underneath are four lists of scrambled sentence parts, which, unscrambled, match the sentence structures of the four sentences. Your task is to match each individual list with its counterpart.

1.   On the blackboard the four rivers of France, drawn with four different colored chalks, had been flowing toward their estuaries for the past three days.
Albert Camus, "The Guest" from Exile and the Kingdom

2.   Dazed, suffering intolerable pain from throat and tongue, with the life half throttled out of him, Buck attempted to face his tormentors.
Jack London, The Call of the Wild

3.   He felt a heavy, sighing peace, like a soldier who has been comfortably wounded and knows that war for him is over.
Edmund Ware, "An Underground Episode"

4.   Six boys came over the hill half an hour early that afternoon, running hard, their heads down, their forearms working, their breath whistling.
John Steinbeck, The Red Pony

Scrambled Sentence Parts

A1. the young pickers
2. about the dance
3. near the orchard
4. had been chatting
5. for their entire lunch break
6. from Wilmont
7. clothed in some simple blue coveralls

B1. now must be guarded
2. of intimacy
3. who has been frequently rejected
4. he spoke
5. like a lover
6. and believes that expressions
7. one slow, cautious sentence

C1. because of vacation
2. comforted
3. in a mood
4. from pressure and performance
5. he started to swing his golf club
6. much improved
7. feeling tremendous relief

D1. their arms up
2. near the fire
3. their bodies writhing
4. just a second sooner that night
5. frenzied dancers spun
6. their voices whispering
7. stomping loudly

PRACTICE 6

The lists underneath the sentences, when unscrambled, will produce sentences identical in structure, but different in content, from the sentences above the list. The lists consist of the *types of structures* (words, phrases, and clauses) that are found in the sentence; and the lists have the same *number of each type of structure.* You are thus provided with two out of the three structural components that occur in the sentence. You must provide the third: *the position of each of the structures.* To do this, refer to the sentence to identify where the author places the words, phrases, and clauses; then, in unscrambling the structurally equivalent sentence, position yours accordingly.

For each sentence there are two separate lists of equivalent sentence parts. The two lists, though structurally identical to each other and to the structure of the model sentence, are different in content. The first list is written in sense language; the second, in nonsense. The purpose of the use of nonsense language is to remove as much meaning as possible from the list of sentence parts. Without the possibility of being distracted by the meaning of each of the sentence parts, you can focus on the major aspect of sentence composing, that is, sentence structure. It will be more helpful to you if you write out the unscrambled versions rather than simply list the correct order of the sentence parts. Doing so will give you practice in writing the various sentence structures. Punctuate correctly, following the punctuation used in the model sentence in each case.

Tom got his lantern, lit it in the hogshead, wrapped it closely in the towel, and the two adventurers crept in the gloom toward the tavern.

Mark Twain, *Tom Sawyer*

1a. ahead of the singer
 b. rehearsed it
 c. Bob wrote his song
 d. but the small orchestra played
 e. sang it beautifully
 f. in the play
 g. in the evenings
 h. with the beat

2a. and the plimey peesto scrunted
 b. broded it
 c. in the tunert
 d. Snaze kurped its blander
 e. crassed it frinkly
 f. of a bleepert
 g. from the marton
 h. with the snart

To carry care to bed is to sleep with a pack on your back.

Thomas Haliburton

3a. in a state
 b. to bring work
 c. of constant worry
 d. is
 e. from the office
 f. to "relax"

4a. in a zipple
 b. to jeld crams
 c. is
 d. near town
 e. from a zapple
 f. to murd

The man who writes about himself and his own time is the only man who writes about all people and about all time.

George Bernard Shaw

5a. with great enthusiasm
 b. a sportscaster
 c. and with solid knowledge
 d. the choice announcer
 e. is
 f. who communicates
 g. who communicates
 h. and sports' top athletes
 i. with fans

6a. and near forty bloops
 b. the blends
 c. the best blends
 d. and their brained nabort
 e. which croak
 f. are
 g. which croak
 h. near thirty bleeps
 i. from selfhoose

A leather handbag, extremely worn, but with a label inside it as impressive as the one inside Mrs. Snell's hat, lay on the pantry.

J.D. Salinger, "Down at the Dinghy" from *Nine Stories*

7a.   very dry
 b.   in Grandma's eyes
 c.   as appealing
 d.   the wrinkled skin
 e.   as the sparkle
 f.   shone in the candlelight
 g.   about it
 h.   yet with a softness

8a.   an oversized saltert
 b.   in its woostem
 c.   quite pritert
 d.   as lumrious
 e.   plazoned from a yambrod
 f.   as a klanion
 g.   on it
 h.   and of a color

PRACTICE 7

The careful ordering of sentence parts to produce good sentences and the careful ordering of sentences to produce good paragraphs are skills worth acquiring, ones which sentence scrambling can help you to achieve.

The following is a scrambled version of the climactic paragraph from Edgar Allan Poe's "The Fall of the House of Usher." It is made up of four lists of scrambled sentences, with Poe's punctuation retained. Each list, when unscrambled, will produce one of the four sentences from Poe's paragraph.

First, unscramble the sentences. As you do, notice how carefully Poe has ordered his sentence parts. Second, unscramble the paragraph—that is, decide which order of the four sentences will produce the best organization for the content of the paragraph. To help, here is an outline of the content.

Sentence One: setting the stage
Sentence Two: introduction of main character
Sentence Three: description of main character
Sentence Four: action of main character

The paragraph, which focuses on the mysterious main character, Lady Madeline of Usher, is the climax of the story.

Unscramble each list of sentence parts to produce one of Poe's sentences. The sentence part that begins the sentence is capitalized. Then unscramble the sentences to produce Poe's paragraph. Write out your paragraph, then compare yours with Poe's in the References.

1a. there *did* stand the lofty and enshrouded figure

  b. but then without those doors

  c. It was the work of the rushing gust—

  d. of the Lady Madeline of Usher

2a. and the evidence of some bitter struggle

  b. There was blood

  c. upon every portion of her emaciated frame

  d. upon her white robes,

3a. there had been found the potency of a spell,

  b. upon the instant,

  c. As if in the superhuman energy of his utterance

  d. the huge antique panels

  e. their ponderous and ebony jaws

  f. to which the speaker pointed

  g. threw slowly back,

4a. to and fro upon the threshold—

  b. bore him to the floor a corpse,

  c. upon the person of her brother,

  d. he had anticipated

  e. then, with a low, moaning cry,

  f. and in her violent and now final death-agonies,

  g. For a moment she remained trembling and reeling

  h. fell heavily inward

  i. and a victim to the terrors

REVIEWING AND APPLYING SENTENCE SCRAMBLING

Variety in sentence structure is a strong characteristic of the writing of professionals. One of the easiest yet most effective ways of achieving sentence structure variety is by repositioning the sentence parts of a sentence already written.

PRACTICE 8

To recognize that sentence parts are movable, do the following Practice. For each list of scrambled sentence parts, unscramble the parts three times, each time producing a sentence with the parts in a different order. Punctuate accordingly. Indicate which of the three versions you consider the most effective arrangement, and explain your choice. Then check the References to compare your choice with the sentence as originally written by the professional writer.

Scrambled Sentence Parts

a.   so coldly burning
b.   falling upon his knees
c.   which was so huge
d.   as he watched the Star
e.   he began to pray humbly

Unscrambled Sentences (Three Versions)

1.   Falling upon his knees as he watched the Star, which was so huge, so coldly burning, he began to pray humbly.
2.   He began to pray humbly, falling upon his knees, as he watched the Star, which was so huge, so coldly burning.
3.   As he watched the Star, which was so huge, so coldly burning, falling upon his knees, he began to pray humbly.

The most effective version is the first. The second is less well organized, with the main actions (praying, falling on his knees) appearing secondary to the description of the Star.

The third version places the phrase *falling upon his knees* in a position in which it seems to describe the Star rather than the person. Here is the sentence as written by the professional:

As he watched the Star, which was so huge, so coldly burning, he began to pray humbly, falling upon his knees.

Taylor Caldwell, *Dear and Glorious Physician*

Taylor Caldwell's sentence differs from all three, but the first version above is equally effective. It is quite possible that the sentence you produce and choose as the best of your three could be as effective as the sentence produced by the professional writer, even if your sentence structure differs from that used by the professional.

1a.   leaving the oak box of money
b.   leaving the quirt
c.   he ran from the place
d.   leaving his suitcase

From a sentence by John Steinbeck, *East of Eden*

2a.   and tight

  b.   a mortgage financier

  c.   the father was respectable

  d.   and forecloser

  e.   and a stern, upright collection-plate passer

From a sentence by O. Henry, "The Ransom of Red Chief"

3a.   for nothing can be done

  b.   after Buck Fanshaw's inquest

  c.   without a public meeting

  d.   a meeting of the short-haired brotherhood was held

  e.   on the Pacific coast

  f.   and an expression of sentiment.

From a sentence by Mark Twain, "Buck Fanshaw's Funeral"

4a.   the littlest

  b.   with them

  c.   I had ever seen

  d.   carrying a gnarled walking stick

  e.   oldest man

  f.   was Elmo Goodhue Pipgrass

From a sentence by Max Shulman, "The Unlucky Winner"

5a.   over long woolen underwear

  b.   he bounded

  c.   around his chest

  d.   out of bed

  e.   and a leather jacket

  f.   wearing a long flannel nightgown

  g.   a nightcap

From a sentence by James Thurber, "The Night the Ghost Got In"

6a.   looked up from his scrambled eggs

  b.   once upon a sunny morning

  c.   who sat in a breakfast nook

  d.   quietly cropping the roses

  e.   with a gold horn

  f.   a man

  g.   to see a white unicorn

  h.   in the garden

From a sentence by James Thurber, "The Unicorn in the Garden"

7a.   grabbed my right foot

  b.   of patent-leather dancing pumps

    c.   then

    d.   and shoved it into one of them

    e.   as a shoehorn

    f.   she removed the gleaming pair

    g.   out of a box on the bed

    h.   using her finger

Jean Shepherd, "Wanda Hickey's Night of Golden Memories"

 8a.   such as weather balloons

    b.   as a general rule

    c.   satellites

    d.   of the World Trade Center

    e.   careful on-the-scene investigations disclose

    f.   meteorites

    g.   that most "unidentified" flying objects are quite ordinary phenomena

    h.   who blew off the roof

    i.   named Lewis Mandelbaum

    j.   and even once a man

Woody Allen, "The UFO Menace"

Not only is it possible to do such repositioning of sentence parts with professionally written sentences, it is quite possible, and quite easy, to reposition sentence parts of your own sentences. Often, experimenting with positioning produces a revised sentence superior to the original sentence, showing greater sophistication of style, demonstrating a better interrelationship in content of one sentence part to another, and varying sentence structures of successive sentences.

PRACTICE 9

Select twenty sentences from several pieces of writing you have done in the past. Choose sentences in which the sentence parts may be repositioned. For each of the twenty, reposition various sentence parts, trying different arrangements. Write two alternate versions for each sentence in which the only change is the repositioning of the sentence parts. Indicate which of the sentence arrangements you prefer and why.

2
Sentence Imitating

DEFINING SENTENCE IMITATING

Sentence imitating is the use of professional writers' sentences as models for writing your own sentences. The structure of your sentence is the same as the model's but the content is different. The purpose is to increase your ability to vary sentence structure through a deliberate imitation of the structure of the model sentence. The ultimate objective, and the objective of all the sentence composing techniques in this book, is mature sentence structure.

Each educated user of the English language learns two kinds of English: speech and writing. Each is learned at a different time. Speech is the first English we learn; writing, the second English. Young children acquire speech by paying close attention to the speech of their parents, older brothers and sisters, and friends. These speakers are actually teachers of the first English to a child, who then models his or her speech upon their example and intuitively learns the "rules" that govern speech, practices them, and eventually becomes a competent speaker. In other words, the first English is acquired through careful imitation of models.

Although they share a common language (English), speech and writing are significantly different. Learning these significant differences is essential if you want to write well. The process that will help you acquire the characteristics associated with good writing is the same process that allowed you to acquire the characteristics of speech—that is, imitation.

With speech, the models were speakers in your environment. Through them you learned the "rules" of the first English. The models through whom you can learn the "rules" of the second English are professional writers. Their sentences are used throughout this book as models for acquiring competence in writing.

Unless you realize that writing is significantly different from speech, you will tend to apply inappropriately the patterns of speech to writing, with often confusing and immature results. Many of the patterns of speech, though appropriate to speech, are highly inappropriate to writing.

19

PRACTICE 1

The purpose here is to illustrate the difference between first English (speech) and second English (writing). In the sentence pairs below, one is an example of speech, the other of writing. All the sentences are from the short story collection *Winesburg, Ohio* by Sherwood Anderson. The spoken sentences are taken from dialogue, chosen for their accurate reflection of the patterns of real speech; the other sentences are from non-dialogue passages, chosen for their reflection of the patterns of competent writing of description or narration. The main difference is in sentence structure. For each pair of sentences, tell which is an example of the first English and which is an example of the second English. Explain your choices.

1a.   He'll hurt someone yet, Elmer will.

  b.   On and on went her voice.

2a.   Over the long field came a thin girlish voice.

  b.   He'd shout at Turk, and Turk would shout at him.

3a.   He ran down the hillside, sobbing as he ran.

  b.   I worked, and at night I went to bed and slept.

4a.   Pouncing upon a bystander, he began to talk.

  b.   He has McKinley bluffed and don't you forget.

5a.   It sat on the back of an express wagon, and they were on the seat as unconcerned as anything.

  b.   Some were amusing, some almost beautiful, and one, a woman all drawn out of shape, hurt the old man by her grotesqueness.

6a.   When Jesse Bentley, absorbed in his own idea, suddenly arose and advanced toward him, his terror grew until his whole body shook.

  b.   Big things are going to be done in the country, and there will be more money to be made than I ever dreamed of.

7a.   He lived with his mother, a grey, silent woman with a peculiar ashy complexion.

  b.   There isn't anything in the house for supper, and you've got to get to town and back in a hurry.

8a.   Even the clothes mother used to wear were not like other people's clothes, and look at that coat in which father goes about there in town, thinking he's dressed up, too.

  b.   Her husband, Tom Willard, a slender, graceful man with square shoulders, a quick military step, and a black mustache trained to turn sharply up at the ends, tried to put the wife out of his mind.

The Practices in this book are based on the fact that writing good sentences can be learned through imitation. In most grammar and composition text-books, this process, ironically, receives little attention. Writing competent sentences can be learned through the deliberate imitation of sentences written by professionals rather than by analyzing the "rules" that govern good writ-ten sentences. Sentence imitating focuses on the differences between speech and writing rather than on the similarities. The model for good writing should be sentences written by professional writers, not speech.

Imitating the structures of professionally written sentences and supply-ing your own content to fill the structures require little knowledge of formal grammar and can result in great improvements in your writing performance.

PRACTICE 2

Structural differences among sentences are not difficult to distinguish. The ability to make such distinctions is important for students who wish to im-prove their sentence composing skills through sentence imitating. This Prac-tice teaches you how to make distinctions among sentence structures.

Below are groups of three sentences. Two of the sentences in each group are identical in structure. The other sentence in the group, although compe-tently written, is structurally different from the other two. Identify the sen-tence that is different. Then, explain how you were able to identify the struc-tures of the other two as identical.

1a.   Great was his care of them.

b.   Something else he saw.

c.   Chilling was her story of passion.

2a.   The big thing, exciting yet frightening, was to talk to her, say what he hoped to do.

b.   There was also a rhino, who, from the tracks and the kicked-up mound of strawy dung, came there each night.

c.   An acceptable solution, simple and efficient, is to negotiate with the management, emphasize what the workers want to delete.

3a.   Much later the accountant finished, ledgers in their vertical files on the right side of the desk, pencils and pens in the container decorated with seals and designs on the shelf above the desk.

b.   This leader, whose word was law among boys who defied authority for the sake of defiance, was no more than twelve or thirteen years old and looked even younger.

c.   Soon afterwards they retired, Mama in her big oak bed on one side of the room, Emilio and Rosy in their boxes full of straw and sheepskins on the other side of the room.

4a. During rush-hour traffic, when his nerves were frazzled, Brent Hammond, twenty miles above the speed limit, hit his brakes, from which came sharp peals and leaden grindings as though the metal were alive and hurting.

b. On stormy nights, when the tide was out, the bay of Fougere, fifty feet below the house, resembled an immense black pit, from which arose mutterings and sighs as if the sands down there had been alive and complaining.

c. Aleck Sander stood out from the shadows, walking, already quite near in the moonless dark, a little taller than Big Ed, though there was only a few months' difference between them.

5a. Listening to evaluate the difference between the two violins, the concertmaster chose, glancing back and forth over the two instruments, the one with the slightly arched bow.

b. Light flickered on bits of ruby glass and on sensitive capillary hairs in the nylon-brushed nostrils of the creature that quivered gently, gently, its eight legs spidered under it on rubber-padded paws.

c. Pretending to take an interest in the New Season's Models, Gumbril made, squinting sideways over the burning tip of his cigar, an inventory of her features.

6a. He reached over for the submachine gun, took the clip out that was in the magazine, felt in his pockets for the clips, opened the action and looked through the barrel, put the clip back in the groove of the magazine until it clicked, and then looked down the hill slope.

b. Amused yet bewildered, near the sardonic boy in a corner of the cafeteria, with a friend who had invited her and another whose boyfriend was his remarkably opposite twin, Joan thought constantly that noon about the ambivalence of her emotions.

c. Abandoned and helpless, under the crude lean-to in the courtyard of the tin factory, beside the woman who had lost a breast and the man whose burned face was scarcely a face any more, Miss Sasaki suffered awfully that night from the pain in her broken leg.

PRACTICING SENTENCE IMITATING

The first task in attempting to imitate the structure of a professionally written sentence is to carefully observe its structure, sentence part by sentence part. Important structural clues can help. One such clue is punctuation. Observing the boundaries of the punctuation marks in the model sentence allows you to focus on one sentence part at a time and to imitate just that part of the sentence. Another helpful clue is the use of certain kinds of words in the model sentence, or parts of words, especially word endings.

Compare these two sentences: the first is a model; the second, an imitation. Notice how the imitation relied on the clues (boldface) of punctuation and certain kinds of words and word endings.

Model

Pretend**ing to** take an interest in **the** New Season's Models, Gumbril made, squint**ing** sideways **over** the burning tip of his cigar, an inventory of her features.

Aldous Huxley, Antic Hay

Imitation

Listen**ing to** evaluate the difference between **the** two violins, the concertmaster chose, glanc**ing** back and forth **over** the two instruments, the one with the slightly arched bow.

Notice the kinds of words and word endings from the model used in the imitation. The words *(structure words)* are not key words from the model; they are words difficult to define *(to, the, over)*. You may use words like them, but don't use key words from the model *(interest, squinting, cigar,* and so forth). In addition, word endings (suffixes) may be used.

Sometimes it's desirable to change the form of a word from the model. For example, if the model uses *is* and you need the plural, you'd use *are;* if the model uses the present tense *(is)* and you need the past tense, you'd use *was.* You can also substitute: if the model uses "*near* the bridge," you might want to use a different preposition—for example, "*with* a pencil."

Review the punctuation patterns in the model and the imitation. They are identical. In doing the imitation, the student worked on one sentence part at a time, concentrating on how that particular sentence part is structured, then imitated only that particular sentence part. The process is then repeated with the next sentence part, then the next, the next, and so forth. Using punctuation marks from the model sentence as the boundary markers for sentence parts, the model has four sentence parts:

First Sentence Part

Model: Pretending to take an interest in the New Season's Models,
Imitation: Listening to evaluate the difference between the two violins,

Second Sentence Part

Model: Gumbril made,
Imitation: the concertmaster chose,

Third Sentence Part

Model: squinting sideways over the burning tip of his cigar,
Imitation: glancing back and forth over the two instruments,

Fourth Sentence Part

Model: an inventory of her features.
Imitation: the one with the slightly arched bow.

Notice that the two sentences are almost identical in structure; however, they are very different in content and somewhat different in length—the imitation uses more words. Duplicating the exact number of words in the model is undesirable. Don't focus on the words; focus, instead, on the structure. Imitate only the structure. You may, however, use some things from the model in your sentence imitation, provided they are of the type described above (namely, structure words or word endings). It is always desirable to use the exact punctuation of the model in your imitation. The use of some of the same words/word endings and the use of the exact punctuation of the model will make sentence imitating easy.

Notice also that almost no grammatical analysis is necessary to imitate sentence structures. The reason is that you already know in an informal way (intuitively) the grammatical word groups to which all of the words in the model sentences belong. As you imitate any given model, you automatically (almost without thinking about it) provide words that are members of the same word groups.

To raise this unconscious grammatical analysis to the conscious level would be very frustrating. For example, consider the following directions for the construction of a sentence you were asked to produce:

Directions: Write a sentence that has the following structure, with the sentence parts arranged in the order in which the structural components are herein listed: Begin with a present participle followed immediately by a noun infinitive serving as the object of the participle. Within this infinitive phrase should be the following, in order: a noun serving as the object of the infinitive, followed by an adjectival prepositional phrase. Next, provide the main clause for the sentence, one consisting of only two words, the first acting as the subject of the clause, the second acting as its verb. Follow the main clause with a present participle modified by a chain of two prepositional phrases, the second of which modifies the object of the first prepositional phrase. Finish your sentence with the direct object of the main clause previously mentioned. Punctuate correctly.

That is a grammatical description of the model sentence by Aldous Huxley. Not only is that kind of direction unnecessary for sentence imitating, it is undesirable and would frustrate even an expert grammarian in trying to produce the sentence with the structural characteristics described. Instead, following the guidelines of sentence imitating described above, the direction is simple: "Write a sentence of your own that has structure similar to the structure in the model sentence but use your own content."

The important thing is to compose good sentences, not to analyze grammar. The best way to learn to write is to write, not to dissect somebody else's sentences. Sentence imitating does rely on somebody else's sentences—those of professional writers—but only as means, not as ends in themselves.

PRACTICE 3

Following the guidelines for sentence imitating mentioned earlier, write an imitation of each of these model sentences. The models have a structure you should already be familiar with through discussion of the same sentences in the last Practice.

1.   Great was his care of them.
Jack London, *All Gold Canyon*

2.   The big thing, exciting yet frightening, was to talk to her, say what he hoped to do.
Bernard Malamud, *The Assistant*

3.   He had never been hungrier, and he filled his mouth with wine, faintly tarry-tasting from the leather bag, and swallowed.
Ernest Hemingway, *For Whom the Bell Tolls*

4.   Soon afterwards they retired, Mama in her big oak bed on one side of the room, Emilio and Rosy in their boxes full of straw and sheepskins on the other side of the room.
John Steinbeck, "Flight"

5.   On stormy nights, when the tide was out, the bay of Fougere, fifty feet below the house, resembled an immense black pit, from which arose mutterings and sighs as if the sands down there had been alive and complaining.
Joseph Conrad, "The Idiots"

To help you, here are sentences imitating the structures of the five model sentences above. The structure words/word endings and punctuation that have been retained from the original sentences are in boldface type.

1.   Chilling **was her** story **of** passion.

2.   An acceptable solution**,** simple and efficient**,** is **to** negotiate **with** the management**,** emphasize **what** the workers want to delete.

3.   The horse had never been nast**ier,** and it threw its riders to the ground, cold and hard from the frost**,** and bolted.

4. Much later the accountant finished, ledgers in their vertical files on the right side of the desk, pencils and pens in their containers decorated with seals and designs on the shelf above the desk.

5. During rush-hour traffic, when his nerves were frazzled, Brent Hammond, twenty miles above the speed limit, hit his brakes, from which came sharp peals and leaden grindings as though the metal were alive and hurting.

Compare #2 in the imitations with its model. In the model two words with *ing* suffixes (*exciting* yet *frightening*) modify the subject of the sentence. The imitation uses two adjectives to modify the subject (*simple* and *efficient*). This kind of substitution is often desirable, for it allows more freedom in word choice.

Compare #3 with its model. In the model one adjective is used at the beginning of this phrase: "faintly *tarry-tasting* from the leather bag." The imitation uses two adjectives at the beginning of the equivalent phrase: "*cold* and *hard* from the frost." Adding structures to those present in the model allows greater flexibility. For example, if the model has one prepositional phrase, you may want to add another one in your imitation; or if a noun is unmodified in the model, you may want to modify it in your imitation.

PRACTICE 4

For each of the four model sentences below, there are two sentence imitations. Each of the sentence imitations approximates the structure of the model. Do three things. First, match the imitations for each model. Next, indicate which words/word endings have been retained in the imitations (these are the structure words/word endings that gave the writers of the imitations clues to the structure). Finally, write an imitation of each model.

After you have matched the sentence imitations to their models, indicate which of these factors helped you the most and which helped you the least: content, structure, words/word endings, sentence length, number of words, and punctuation.

Models

1. Near the spot upriver to which Mr. Tanimoto had transported the priests, there sat a large case of rice cakes which a rescue party had evidently brought for the wounded lying thereabouts but hadn't distributed.

John Hersey, Hiroshima

2. There was also a rhino, who, from the tracks and the kicked-up mound of strawy dung, came there each night.

Ernest Hemingway, Green Hills of Africa

3. The dark silence was there and the heavy shapes, sitting, and the little blue light burning.

Ray Bradbury, The Vintage Bradbury

4.   Light flickered on bits of ruby glass and on sensitive capillary hairs in the nylon-brushed nostrils of the creature that quivered gently, gently, its eight legs spidered under it on rubber-padded paws.
Ray Bradbury, Fahrenheit 451

Imitations

a.   Stars twinkled on pieces of broken shells and on ruined sand castles in the sea-drenched sand of the beach that stretched miles, endless miles, its many shells strewn on it by high-crested waves.

b.   At the place in the room where he had left his books, there was a stack of journals that had evidently been brought by several of the more academic students but hadn't been used by the teacher.

c.   The dense fog was there and the bloody bodies, dying, and the torn white flag waving.

d.   I sat on velvet grass and under spreading blue leaves in the light-yellow atmosphere of a planet that orbited, slowly, steadily, its six moons clinging close like new-born children.

e.   There was also a turtle, who, from the half-eaten tomato and the hole under the fence, had visited the garden that day.

f.   The big race was ready to begin and the line of cars, waiting, and the red flag still standing.

g.   There was also the horror, which, from the odor and snake-belly sensation of dead flesh, came there each time.

h.   Outside the shack from which the patrol had started shooting, there was a blast of gunfire that the rebels had intended for the door lock but hadn't hit.

PRACTICE 5

Each of the following three paragraphs was written by a student. The sentences lack structural variety. Point out what makes them monotonously alike.

1. Many people envied this house for its size and majesty. 2. The large iron door with its carved designs looked like a barrier to the outside world. 3. The stained glass window looked like a new bright rainbow. 4. The intricate wood carvings around the windows and ledges looked priceless. 5. The roof was in the shape of a dome. 6. The gold weathervane at the top gleamed in the bright sun.

1. The house was nauseating to look at. 2. It was painted a revolting shade of pink. 3. The clothes line hung from the chimney to the television antenna on the roof revealing the wardrobe of the entire family. 4. The shutters that hid

the windows needed something to hide themselves. 5. They were painted an obnoxious shade of red that clashed greatly with the overall color of the house. 6. The flower boxes were filled with detestable plants such as cactus and plants with only thorns. 7. The house was indeed the sore thumb of the block.

1. A horse is a very peculiar animal. 2. He is a lot like a person. 3. He has a soft furry body in the winter, and when summer comes it becomes slick and shiny. 4. His face is kind looking. 5. His eyes set back in his head funny, while his nose is as soft as velvet. 6. His mane and tail hang long and fine, while his feet are hard and sturdy.

PRACTICE 6

Here are two more paragraphs, this time almost identical in content but very different structurally. One is from Anne Morrow Lindbergh's *Gift from the Sea;* the other is a paraphrase of hers, written in a style typical of many students. Point out which was written by Lindbergh. Justify your choice by reference to the sentence structures of each paragraph.

Paragraph One

1. I have a round, full, glossy snail shell. 2. I am holding it in my hand, and it is comfortable and compact. 3. It looks milky, opaque, and pinkish. 4. It has a perfect spiral on its smooth face. 5. This spiral circles around to the center of the shell. 6. The center looks like the pupil of an eye. 7. I am looking at this eye in the center, and it seems to be looking at me too.

Paragraph Two

1. This is a snail shell, round, full, and glossy as a horse chestnut. 2. Comfortable and compact, it sits curled up like a cat in the hollow of my hand. 3. Milky and opaque, it has the pinkish bloom of the sky on a summer evening, ripening to rain. 4. On its smooth, symmetrical face is pencilled with precision a perfect spiral, winding inward to the pin point center of the shell, the tiny dark core of the apex, the pupil of the eye. 5. It stares at me, this mysterious single eye—and I stare back.

It is relatively easy to identify Lindbergh's paragraph, relying totally on the mature and varied sentence structures she uses in contrast to the monotonous sentence structures of the other paragraph.

PRACTICE 7

Here are six paragraphs, all with the same number of sentences (five). Three are student imitations of Lindbergh's paragraph. Identify these three and then point out the major differences in sentence structure between the imitations and the remaining three paragraphs.

Paragraph One

1. The school bus pulled up and let the children out. 2. One of the little boys was running after his dog. 3. The dog had followed him to school and refused to go home when the boy chased him. 4. The other students thought it was funny when the dog ran into the school building. 5. Somebody had left the door open on purpose.

Paragraph Two

1. When it snowed yesterday, I was at the library. 2. The library is one near where I live and has many books that can help a lot with the assignments from school. 3. A lot of my friends go there to visit with each other and to do some research and studying. 4. The librarians are helpful when you need to find some book to do a history or English assignment. 5. I like the library!

Paragraph Three

1. There is a snowflake, light, delicate, and fluffy as a piece of cotton. 2. Swirling and blowing, it floats down from the sky like the seeds of the milkweed plant. 3. White and bright, it has the gleam of the blinding sunlight and the reflecting moonlight, shining in silver. 4. On its surface is stenciled a star, formed with its five or six symmetrical points, the arms of the snowflake, the body of it. 5. It falls to earth, this crystal of beauty—and the earth melts it.

Paragraph Four

1. This is an old book, interesting, long, but thought-provoking as a philosophical treatise. 2. Soiled but well read, it remains standing upright on my bookshelf mixed in with paperbacks. 3. Analytic and probing, it reveals many pitfalls in the process of thinking, describing wrong conclusions. 4. In its yellow pages are recorded with skill many criticisms, converging ultimately into the story of all people, the universal, timeless tale of every individual, the discourse on humanity. 5. It speaks of man, this lengthy discourse—yet man ignores it.

Paragraph Five

1. Some rock stars are very colorful and exciting to watch when they perform at a live concert. 2. Usually hundreds or thousands of teenagers attend these concerts, which are usually held in large convention halls or sometimes outdoors in large parks or other public places. 3. Music-lovers look forward to

attending these exciting events. 4. Despite what many people say, the behavior at the concerts is very good. 5. It is noisy, but since noise is what anyone would expect at such concerts, nobody there really minds.

Paragraph Six

1. This is a room, dark, comfortable, and at times lonely as a silent cave. 2. Small and private, it can absorb my thoughts like a sponge. 3. Comfortable and secure, the room has a feeling of safety and peace, providing a hiding place. 4. On its walls are varicolored posters, all reflecting moods of mine, ranging from joy to despair. 5. The posters face me, those mirrors of my soul—and I reminisce.

As you can see, it is possible to put an unlimited variety of content in the same sentence structure. In the three imitations, the structures are the same—the same sentence parts, the same punctuation.

Remember that in sentence imitating it is not necessary to duplicate the sentence structure of the model exactly. Notice in the imitation sentences above that some add structures that were not in the model, some make changes in the structure, and some drop structures that were in the model. All of the imitations are, however, enough like the model in sentence structure to be acceptable sentence imitations.

PRACTICE 8

Write a five-sentence descriptive paragraph. Model your sentence structures after those of Lindbergh's description of the snail shell. You may choose anything to describe—a writing instrument, an old family picture, a pet, a sports player in action. Or, use one of the four starter sentences below. If you choose one of these sentences, use it as your first sentence of the paragraph.

1. This is an attic, musty, dark, and forbidding as London fog.
2. This is an eye, glassy, bloodshot, and unfocused as a bad camera shot.
3. This is a crystal goblet, sparkling, clear, and dazzling as a diamond.
4. Here is a baby, soft, warm, and pink as a rose.

REVIEWING AND APPLYING SENTENCE IMITATING

In order to imitate the structures of professionally written sentences, you must first be able to recognize the structural characteristics of the sentence parts contained within the sentence to be imitated. To do this, read the model sentence several times, sentence part by sentence part, noticing the structure words used and the pattern of punctuation.

PRACTICE 9

From the two sentences (A and B) following each model sentence, select the one that approximates the sentence structure of the model; then write a sentence imitation of the model. All models are from *The Martian Chronicles* by Ray Bradbury.

1.   One minute it was Ohio winter, with doors closed, windows locked, the panes blind with frost, icicles fringing every roof, children skiing on slopes, housewives lumbering like great black bears in their furs along the icy streets.

A.   Near the race track where the Derby was held, a peanut vendor, with wrinkled skin, a face like an eagle, boldly stood almost directly in the line of the huge traffic, hawking his peanuts, describing their superb taste, rich aroma.

B.   Yesterday it was the Boston Marathon, with crowds gathered, police ready, the runners covered with suntan oils, many limbering up, even wheelchair participants checking their equipment like careful auto mechanics with their tools of all sorts.

2.   Named but unnamed, and borrowing from humans everything but humanity, the robots stared at the nailed lids of their labeled F.O.B. boxes, in a death that was not even a death, for there had never been a life.

A.   With the carousel slide projector carefully placed atop several books to provide the right height for perfect screen projection, with the slides placed within it, the right organization for the presentation, the lesson began.

B.   Hesitant but not uncertain, and drawing from libraries all of her knowledge, she walked into the room for her comprehensive examination, with a feeling that was certainly not calm, because there would always be the unknown.

3.   Here and there a fire, forgotten in the last rush, lingered and in a sudden access of strength fed upon the dry bones of some littered shack.

A.   Once or twice the siren, obscured by the sudden explosion, echoed but with a dreadful parody of itself sounded with a noise like a banshee.

B.   Now and then, he tweaked his painted, bulbous nose, and the children nearby giggled at the bicycle-horn sound.

PRACTICE 10

Write an imitation of each of the model sentences below.

1.   One of these dogs, the best one, had disappeared.

Fred Gipson, *Old Yeller*

2.   Among the company was a lawyer, a young man of about twenty-five.

Anton Chekhov, "The Bet"

3.   Halfway there he heard the sound he dreaded, the hollow, rasping cough of a horse.

John Steinbeck, *The Red Pony*

4.   Poppa, a good quiet man, spent the last hours before our parting moving aimlessly about the yard, keeping to himself and avoiding me.

Gordon Parks, "My Mother's Dream for Me"

5.   Buck stood and looked on, the successful champion, the dominant primordial beast who had made his kill and found it good.

Jack London, *The Call of the Wild*

6.   He was a jerkline skinner, the prince of the ranch, capable of driving ten, sixteen, even twenty mules with a single line to the leaders.

John Steinbeck, *Of Mice and Men*

7.   Standing in the truck bed, holding onto the bars of the sides, rode the others, twelve-year-old Ruthie and ten-year-old Winfield, grime-faced and wild, their eyes tired but excited, their fingers and the edges of their mouths black and sticky from licorice whips, whined out of their father in town.

John Steinbeck, *The Grapes of Wrath*

8.   The rest were standing around in hatless, smoky little groups of twos and threes and fours inside the heated waiting room, talking in voices that, almost without exception, sounded collegiately dogmatic, as though each young man, in his strident, conversational turn, was clearing up, once and for all, some highly controversial issue, one that the outside, non-matriculating world had been bungling, provocatively or not, for centuries.

J. D. Salinger, *Franny and Zooey*

Sentence imitating is certainly not an end in itself. The goal of sentence imitating is to allow you to become very familiar with the structural possibilities for composing sentences through careful attention to the ways in which professional writers structure their sentences. The variety of sentence structure possibilities is endless. In this section of the book only a small portion of those possibilities has been shown. Through the Practices you should have become aware of those possibilities. This awareness is crucial to the ultimate goal of sentence imitating: writing sentences structured in mature, varied ways, similar to those of professional writers, but *without* the use of model sentences. In other words, sentence imitating is designed to provide a means for your independent use of sentence structure variety in your own writing. Having learned what sentence structure variety is possible, you can now apply this knowledge in your own writing.

PRACTICE 11

Write an original paragraph five to ten sentences in length. Include somewhere in the paragraph a sentence imitation of as many of the following model sentences as you can. Even if you use only one or two model sentences for imitation, in the rest of your paragraph try to write sentences (without the use of models) that are similar in structure to those associated with professional writing.

1. Over this rocky area relieved by a few shady tall persimmon trees the graduating class walked.

Maya Angelou, I Know Why the Caged Bird Sings

2. A few hours before, he adored me, was devoted and worshipful, and now he was angry.

Anaïs Nin, The Diary of Anaïs Nin

3. Behind a billboard, on an empty lot, he opened the purse and saw a pile of silver and copper coins.

Charles Chaplin, My Autobiography

4. The frozen earth thawed, leaving the short grass looking wet and weary.

Peter Abraham, Tell Freedom

5. I was fourteen at the time, too young for a full-time job, but I managed to get a Bronx Home News route, for which I paid five dollars a week.

Milton Kaplan, Commentary

6. In my robe and barefoot in the backyard, under cover of going to see about my new beans, I gave myself up to the gentle warmth and thanked God that no matter what evil I had done in my life He had allowed me to live to see this day.

Maya Angelou, I Know Why the Caged Bird Sings

7. Certainly no one was strong enough to control them, least of all their mother, the queen-bee of the hive, on whom nine-tenths of the burden fell, on whose strength they all depended, but whose children were much too self-willed and self-confident to take guidance from her, or from any one else, unless in the direction they fancied.

Henry Adams, The Education of Henry Adams

PRACTICE 12

Write a composition of two to five paragraphs. Include somewhere in the composition sentence imitations of two of the above model sentences: one chosen from the list of short model sentences (# 1–5) and the other from the list of longer model sentences (#6 and #7). Do not use the same model sentence you used in the last Practice. Even though you will be using only two model sentences for two sentence imitations, in the rest of the sentences in your composition try to write sentence structures (without the use of models) that are similar to the sentence structures associated with professional writing. In structure, all of your sentences, not just the two imitations, should resemble those structures associated with the sentences of professional writers.

3
Sentence Combining

DEFINING SENTENCE COMBINING

Sentence combining is the process of integrating two or more related sentences into one sentence. Unlike sentence scrambling and sentence imitating, in which you were given the structure for the sentence parts, sentence combining provides only the content. You provide the sentence structure in which to express that content, thereby contributing one-half of the resulting sentence. Since the goal of this book is to teach you the characteristics that determine good sentence structure, your work here in sentence combining will help you reach that goal.

There are three types of sentence combining: joining, inserting, and changing. They may be used individually or together, depending on the particular sentence combining task. Regardless of which type is used, the goal is the same: to produce smooth, economical, mature writing through the use of one, rather than more than one, sentence.

Sentence Combining through Joining

One sentence is connected to another with no changes made in the original sentences. There are two ways commonly used to make the connection.

Use of a Semicolon

Two sentences (rarely more than two) having related content are written as one, with a semicolon—never a comma—joining them.

Multi-Sentence Version: Fenella hardly ever saw her grandma with her head uncovered. She looked strange.
Single-Sentence Version: Fenella hardly ever saw her grandma with her head uncovered; she looked strange.

Katherine Mansfield, "The Voyage"

Multi-Sentence Version: Execution kills instantly. Life imprisonment kills by degrees.
Single-Sentence Version: Execution kills instantly; life imprisonment kills by degrees.

Anton Chekov, "The Bet"

Multi-Sentence Version: A moment passed. Gregor lay stretched there. Around all was still. Perhaps that was a good sign.
Single-Sentence Version: A moment passed; Gregor lay stretched there; around all was still; perhaps that was a good sign. (Rare)

Franz Kafka, *The Metamorphosis*

Use of a Comma Plus **and, but, or**

These three words (and, but, or) are called coordinating conjunctions; they join two sentences into one. The conjunction chosen should show the proper relationship between the main ideas joined in the sentence: *and* shows addition; *but* shows contrast; *or* shows alternative or outcome. A comma should be used before coordinating conjunctions.

Multi-Sentence Version: The sun was setting when the truck came back. The earth was bloody in its setting light.
Single-Sentence Version (, and): The sun was setting when the truck came back, **and** the earth was bloody in its setting light.

John Steinbeck, *The Grapes of Wrath*

Multi-Sentence Version: From the windows of his own room he could not see directly into the barnyard where the farm hands had now all assembled to do the morning chores. He could hear the voices of the men and the neighing of the horses.
Single-Sentence Version (, but): From the windows of his own room he could not see directly into the barnyard where the farm hands had now all assembled to do the morning chores, **but** he could hear the voices of the men and the neighing of the horses.

Sherwood Anderson, *Winesburg, Ohio*

Multi-Sentence Version: You drag your past with you everywhere. It drags you.
Single-Sentence Version (, or): You drag your past with you everywhere, **or** it drags you.

James Baldwin, "Every Good-bye Ain't Gone"

Sentence Combining through Inserting

Part of one sentence is inserted in an appropriate position in another sentence. The effect is improved economy of word usage: repetitious elements are removed from one sentence, and the remaining content is inserted into the other sentence. This process is quite common in this section on sentence combining and is frequently done with inserts from several sentences combined into one sentence.

Multi-Sentence Version: He paused. He was puffing noisily.
Single-Sentence Version: He paused, puffing noisily.

John Steinbeck, The Red Pony

Multi-Sentence Version: His head was aching. His throat was sore. He forgot to light the cigarette.
Single-Sentence Version: His head aching, his throat sore, he forgot to light the cigarette.

Sinclair Lewis, Cass Timberlane

Multi-Sentence Version: Bernard was waiting outside. He was waiting on the landing. He was wearing three things. One was a sweater. It was a turtleneck. It was black. Another was flannels. They were dirty. The third thing was slippers.
Single-Sentence Version: Bernard, wearing a black turtleneck sweater, dirty flannels, and slippers, was waiting on the landing outside.

Brian Moore, The Lonely Passion of Judith Hearne

Sentence Combining through Changing

Unlike the previous examples in which no words were changed but some were dropped, in the next examples words are changed as well as dropped. The changes involve either a substitution of one word for another or a change in the grammatical form of the same word. The changes are usually slight, but they are necessary to insure that the resulting sentence, from two or more sentences, is smooth and grammatically correct.

Multi-Sentence Version: Their cabins looked neat and snug. This occurred in the frosty December dusk. Their cabins had pale blue smoke. The smoke rose from the chimneys and doorways. The chimneys and doorways glowed amber from the fires inside.
Single-Sentence Version: In the frosty December dusk, their cabins looked neat and snug with pale blue smoke rising from the chimneys and doorways glowing amber from the fires inside.

Harper Lee, To Kill a Mockingbird

In this example, one of the words *(had)* is changed to a different word in the single-sentence version *(with)*. Two of the words *(rose, glowed)* are changed to different grammatical forms of the same words in the single-sentence version *(rising, glowing)*. The changes provide smoothness and grammatical correctness in the single-sentence version.

PRACTICE 1

Each of the lists of sentences below was derived from a single sentence written by a professional writer. Your task is to combine all of the sentences into just one sentence. Punctuate correctly. After you complete this Practice, compare your sentence with the sentence as it was written by the professional writer. (See the References.)

   Caution: Avoid sentence combining through joining in these Practices. In professional writing, of course, and in your own, coordinating conjunctions and semicolons are used often, but for the purpose of this Practice, stick to sentence combining through inserting or changing, or a combination of the two. Both will help you develop a greater variety of sentence structure in your writing.

1a.   The eyes rolled wide their lids.

b.   The eyes were made of marble.

c.   The lids were made of rubber.
From a sentence by Ray Bradbury, The Martian Chronicles

2a.   The boy watched.

b.   During the watching, his eyes did something.

c.   His eyes were bulging.

d.   All of this occurred in the dark.
From a sentence by Edmund Ware, "An Underground Episode"

3a.   One of the dogs had done something.

b.   It had disappeared.

c.   This dog was the best one of all the dogs.
From a sentence by Fred Gipson, Old Yeller

4a.   The huge eye glittered before me.

b.   The eye was on the right side of its head.

c.   The head was anguished.

d.   The eye was like a cauldron.

e.   I felt that I might drop into that cauldron-eye.

f.   As I dropped, I would be screaming.
From a sentence by Ray Bradbury, "The Fog Horn"

5a.   Doctor Parcival began to walk up and down.

b.   Just before this he jumped to his feet.

c.   Just before this he broke off the tale.

d.   The office in which he walked was of the *Winesburg Eagle.*

e.   In that office someone sat.

f.   The someone was George Willard.

g.   As George sat, he was listening.
From a sentence by Sherwood Anderson, Winesburg, Ohio

6a. This land was waterless.

b. It was furred with cacti.

c. The cacti could store water.

d. In addition, the land was furred with the great-rooted brush.

e. The brush could reach deep into the earth.

f. The brush would do this to get a little moisture.

g. The brush could get along on very little moisture.

From a sentence by John Steinbeck, *The Pearl*

7a. It glided through.

b. As it glided, it brushed the twigs.

c. The twigs were overhanging.

d. It disappeared from the river.

e. It disappeared like some creature.

f. The creature was slim.

g. The creature was amphibious.

h. The creature was leaving the water.

i. The creature was going for its lair.

j. The lair was in the forests.

From a sentence by Joseph Conrad, "The Lagoon" from *Tales of Unrest*

De-combining professionally-written sentences provides much insight into the writing process. It rarely matters whether the original sentence is short, medium, or long. Here are three professionally written sentences, one of each length, with the lists of sentences resulting from sentence de-combining:

Sentence De-Combining: Short Sentence

Silently, desperately, he fought with all his weapons.

Katherine Anne Porter, *Ship of Fools*

1. He fought.
2. The fighting was with weapons.
3. The weapons were his.
4. All of his weapons were used.
5. The fighting was done silently.
6. The fighting was done desperately.

Sentence De-Combining: Medium Sentence

Once his back happened to be half turned toward the door, and, hearing a noise there, he wheeled and sprang up, uttering a loud cry.

Stephen Crane, "The Blue Hotel"

1. Once something happened.
2. What happened was that his back happened to be half turned.
3. His back was half turned toward the door.
4. During this time he heard a noise there.
5. Upon hearing it, he wheeled.
6. Upon hearing it, he sprang up.
7. During the wheeling and the springing up, he was doing something.
8. He was uttering a loud cry.

Sentence De-Combining: Long Sentence

He backed Jack up against the ropes, measured him and then hooked the left very light to the side of Jack's head and socked the right into the body as hard as he could sock, just as low as he could get it.

Ernest Hemingway, "Fifty Grand"

1. He backed Jack up.
2. The backing was against the ropes.
3. He measured him.
4. Then he hooked the left.
5. The hook was very light.
6. The hook was to the side of the head.
7. The head was Jack's.
8. He socked the right.
9. He socked it into the body.
10. The socking was as hard as he could sock.
11. The socking was as low as he could get it.

Of course, Katherine Anne Porter, Stephen Crane, and Ernest Hemingway didn't choose to design their sentences in such ways. The advantages of the original version, each author's actual sentence, over a list of sentences are obvious. Readability is one. The author's sentence is easier to read than a list. Fluency, or smoothness, is another. The flow of ideas is smoother in the author's sentence, where sentence structure helps the reader make quick connections between one idea and the next. Maturity of style is still another reason. It takes a lot of practice to manipulate sentence structures in the ways that these three authors have; almost anyone is capable of writing sentence structures like those in the lists of sentences.

PRACTICE 2

Study the three examples of sentence de-combining above. Notice how several of the sentences in the list were derived from one sentence part of the author's sentence, how the next group was derived from the next sentence part of the author's sentence, and so forth. The purpose of this Practice is to focus on how a skillful writer packs a lot into one sentence.

In this Practice, de-combine each of the sentences below, one sentence part at a time, to produce two or more sentences for each sentence part in the original. The number of sentences you can list is not fixed. Try for more rather than fewer sentences. In doing so, you will become more conscious of the greater economy, variety, and therefore maturity of the original sentence. This awareness should help you improve your own sentence composing.

After you have completed your lists of sentences, set your work aside for a few days. Then, using your lists, combine the sentences and compare your combination with the author's sentence. This added task will help greatly in reinforcing the purposes of this Practice.

1.   The fixer got up on his raw hands and bleeding knees and went on, blindly crawling across the yard.

Bernard Malamud, The Fixer

2.   She flicked her wrist neatly out of Doctor Harry's pudgy careful fingers and pulled the sheet up to her chin.

Katherine Anne Porter, "The Jilting of Granny Weatherall"

3.   On the table, covered with oilcloth figured with clusters of blue grapes, a place was set, and he smelled hot coffee-cake of some kind.

Willa Cather, "Neighbor Rosicky"

4.   Every old woman was a doctor, and gathered her own medicines in the woods, and knew how to compound doses that would stir the vitals of a cast-iron dog.

Mark Twain, Mark Twain's Autobiography

5.   She cleared away the smoking things, then drew back the cotton bedspread from the bed she had been sitting on, took off her slippers, and got into bed.

J. D. Salinger, Franny and Zooey

6.   The driver of the car stopped it, slamming it to a skidding halt on the greasy pavement without warning, actually flinging the two passengers forward until they caught themselves with their braced hands against the dash.

William Faulkner, "Delta Autumn"

7.   The first wave carried with it men accustomed to spaces and coldness and being alone, the coyote and cattlemen, with no fat on them, with faces the years had worn the flesh off, with eyes like nailheads, and hands like the material of old gloves, ready to touch anything.

Ray Bradbury, The Martian Chronicles

PRACTICING SENTENCE COMBINING

There are many ways to combine a group of sentences that are related in content, but not all ways are equally effective. A skillful writer mentally selects the one way out of the many possible combinations that will produce the best sentence. The selection of the best way depends upon many factors: what idea the writer wants to emphasize, what organization of ideas will produce the clearest meaning, and what sentence structure will produce a pleasing variety in the sentences that come before and after.

List of Sentences

1. The carpenter came into the writer's room.
2. The carpenter had been a soldier in the Civil War.
3. The carpenter sat down to talk.
4. He wanted to talk about building a platform.
5. The purpose of the platform was to raise the bed.

Possible Combinations

A. To talk about building a platform to raise the bed, the carpenter, a former Civil War soldier, came into the writer's room and sat down.

B. The carpenter came into the writer's room and sat down to talk, he had been a soldier in the Civil War wanting to talk about building a platform to raise the bed.

C. A former Civil War soldier, the carpenter came into the writer's room and sat down to talk, the talk being about building a platform to raise the bed.

D. The carpenter wanted to talk about building a platform to raise the bed, so he, who had been in the Civil War, came into the writer's room and sat down.

Two of the above are clearly unacceptable: one, because it is really two sentences incorrectly joined by a comma; the other, because it is uneconomical in word usage. Identify these two.

Of the two remaining, which is more effective? Why? Compare the best sentence with the way it was written by the author. Which is better? Why?

The carpenter, who had been a soldier in the Civil War, came into the writer's room and sat down to talk of building a platform for the purpose of raising the bed.

Sherwood Anderson, *Winesburg, Ohio*

PRACTICE 3

Combine each list of sentences twice to produce two different sentences. Punctuate correctly. Indicate which of the two is more effective, and briefly explain the reasons for your choice.

In this Practice you need not necessarily stick to the order of ideas in the list. You may use any arrangement you think will produce a good sentence. Compare your best sentence with the author's in the References. Which is better? Why?

1a. The house was most enjoyable.

  b. The house was in the country.

  c. The enjoyment of the house was on a particular afternoon.

  d. The afternoon was wintry.
Based on a sentence by James Thurber, "The Owl in the Attic"

2a. The earth was bloody in the setting light.

  b. The bloodiness was caused by the sun.

  c. The sun was setting.

  d. At the same time, the truck came back.
Based on a sentence by John Steinbeck, The Grapes of Wrath

3a. He moves nervously.

  b. He moves fast.

  c. His movement, however, has a restraint.

  d. The restraint suggests that he is a cautious man.

  e. The restraint suggests that he is a thoughtful man.
Based on a sentence by John Hersey, Hiroshima

4a. The girls stood aside.

  b. The very small children rolled in the dust.

  c. Some children clung to the hands of their older brothers or sisters.

  d. The girls were doing two things.

  e. They looked over their shoulders at the boys.

  f. They talked among themselves.
Based on a sentence by Shirley Jackson, "The Lottery"

5a. The cake was shaped in a frying pan.

  b. He took flour.

  c. He took oil.

  d. He shaped them into a cake.

  e. The stove functioned on gas.

  f. The gas was bottled.

  g. He lighted the stove.

  h. The stove was little.
Based on a sentence by Albert Camus, "The Guest," from Exile and the Kingdom

6a. He set the cake on the windowsill.

  b. The purpose was to cool it.

  c. He did this after the cake was done.

  d. He heated some milk.

  e. The milk was condensed.

f. The milk was diluted with water.

g. He beat up the eggs.

h. The eggs were beaten into an omelette.
   Based on a sentence by Albert Camus, "The Guest," from *Exile and the Kingdom*

7a. One of the travelers napped upon his cane.

b. The napping was done fitfully.

c. The traveler was the fifth traveler.

d. He sat across the aisle.

e. He sat next to the middle door there.

f. He was a gentleman.

g. He was old.

h. He was withered.
   Based on a sentence by Henry Sydnor Harrison, "Miss Hinch"

Even though the basic unit of all writing is the sentence, writing rarely consists of just one sentence. The next basic unit, consisting of a series of related sentences, is a paragraph. In the next Practice you will combine sentences to produce a paragraph.

PRACTICE 4

Each list of sentences is the basis for one sentence of a paragraph. When each of the lists has been combined, one sentence per list of sentences, you will have produced a paragraph in which all of the sentences are related in content. You can then compare your result with the paragraph as written by the professional author. Evaluate both. If the author's is better, note the reason. As a general guideline, the number of words contained in the author's sentence (the sentence from which the list of sentences was derived) is indicated. You should not necessarily aim for exact duplication of this number. Instead, try to approximate it.

Paragraph for Example: Description of a Snail Shell (five sentences)

1a. This is a snail shell.

b. It is round.

c. It is full.

d. It is glossy.

e. The gloss is like a horse chestnut.

Word Count: thirteen (short sentence)

2a. The shell is comfortable.

b. The shell is compact.

    c.   It sits curled up.

    d.   It sits in the hollow of my hand.

    e.   It sits curled up like a cat.

Word Count: sixteen (medium sentence)

3a.   It is milky.

  b.   It is opaque.

  c.   It has a pinkish bloom.

  d.   The bloom is like the sky on an evening.

  e.   The evening is in summer.

  f.   The evening sky is ripening.

  g.   The ripening is to rain.

Word Count: eighteen (medium sentence)

4a.   A spiral is pencilled on its face.

  b.   The face is smooth.

  c.   The face is symmetrical.

  d.   The spiral is pencilled with precision.

  e.   The spiral winds inward to the center.

  f.   The center is a pinpoint.

  g.   The pinpoint is of the center of the shell.

  h.   The center is the core.

  i.   The core is tiny.

  j.   The core is of the apex.

  k.   The core is the pupil of the eye.

Word Count: thirty-two (long sentence)

5a.   It stares at me.

  b.   It is this mysterious eye.

  c.   I stare back.

Word Count: eleven (short sentence)

Possible Combinations

A.   (1) This is a snail shell which is round, full, and has gloss like a horse chestnut. (2) The shell is comfortable and compact and sits curled up like a cat in the hollow of my hand. (3) It is milky and opaque with a pinkish bloom like the sky on a summer evening when it is ripening to rain. (4) A spiral is pencilled with precision on its smooth symmetrical face, the spiral winding inward to the pinpoint center of the shell, which is a tiny core, an apex, like the pupil of the eye. (5) When this mysterious eye stares at me, I stare back.

B.　(1) This round, full snail shell has a gloss which is like a horse chestnut. (2) It sits in the hollow of my hand because it is comfortable and compact. (3) With its milky and opaque pinkish bloom, it is like a summer evening's sky when it is ripening to rain. (4) The smooth symmetrical pencilled spiral on its face winds inward to the center of the shell, which is its pinpoint or apex or core, like the pupil of the eye. (5) I stare at it with my mysterious eye when it stares at me.

Author's Paragraph

C.　(1) This is a snail shell, round, full, and glossy as a horse chestnut. (2) Comfortable and compact, it sits curled up in the hollow of my hand like a cat. (3) Milky and opaque, it has the pinkish bloom of the sky on a summer evening, ripening to rain. (4) On its smooth symmetrical face is pencilled with precision a spiral, winding inward to the pinpoint center of the shell, the tiny dark core of the apex, the pupil of the eye. (5) It stares at me, this mysterious eye—and I stare back.

Anne Morrow Lindbergh, *Gift from the Sea*

Which paragraph differs in meaning from the intended meaning of the author's paragraph? Cite examples. Which paragraph is inferior in sentence structure to the author's paragraph? Where in the sentences—the beginning, the middle, or the end—is the difference most noticeable? Which paragraph is less economical in use of words than the author's paragraph?

Do a sentence-by-sentence comparison of the sentences in the author's paragraph and the sentences in the other two paragraphs. For each sentence, list the characteristics of the author's sentence that make it superior to either of the two sentences from the other two paragraphs. Focus on three things in your comparison: meaning, sentence structure, and economy.

Paragraph One

Description of a Valley in California in December from "The Chrysanthemums" by John Steinbeck (five sentences)

1a.　The fog closed off the Salinas Valley.
b.　The fog was high.
c.　The fog was like gray flannel.
d.　The fog was of winter.
e.　It closed off the Salinas Valley from two things.
f.　One was from the sky.
g.　The other was from all the rest of the world.

Word Count: twenty-three (medium sentence)

2a.   The fog sat on every side of the mountains.
b.   The fog was like a lid on the mountains.
c.   The fog made something out of the great valley.
d.   The fog made the great valley into a closed pot.
Word Count: twenty (medium sentence)

3a.   On the land floor the gang plows bit deep.
b.   The land floor was broad.
c.   The land floor was level.
d.   The gang plows left the earth shining.
e.   The earth was black.
f.   The shining was like metal where the shares had cut.
Word Count: twenty-four (medium sentence)

4a.   The yellow stubble fields seemed to be bathed in something.
b.   The something was pale cold sunshine.
c.   The stubble fields were on the foothill ranches.
d.   The foothill ranches were across the Salinas River.
e.   The pale cold sunshine was an illusion.
f.   There was no sunshine in the valley now in December.
Word Count: thirty-two (long sentence)

5a.   The willow scrub flamed.
b.   The willow scrub was thick.
c.   The willow scrub was along the river.
d.   The willow scrub flamed with yellow leaves.
e.   The yellow leaves were sharp.
f.   The yellow leaves were positive.
Word Count: fourteen (short sentence)

Paragraph Two

Description and Explanation of a Native African Bushman Dance from *The Harmless People* by Elizabeth Marshall Thomas (four sentences)

1a.   To have a dance the women do certain things.
b.   They sit in a circle.
c.   Their babies are on their backs.
d.   Their babies are asleep.
e.   The women sing medicine songs.

f. The songs are sung in several parts.

g. The songs are sung in falsetto voices.

h. During the singing the women clap their hands.

i. The clapping is done in rhythm.

j. The rhythm is sharp.

k. The rhythm is staccato.

l. The rhythm is at counterpoint to the rhythm of their voices.

Word Count: forty-four (long sentence)

2a. The men dance behind their backs.

b. The men dance one behind the other.

c. The men circle slowly around.

d. The men take steps.

e. The steps are very short.

f. The steps are pounding.

g. The steps are at counterpoint to the rhythms.

h. One of the rhythms is the rhythm of the singing.

i. The other rhythm is the rhythm of the clapping.

Word Count: thirty-three (long sentence)

3a. Now and then the men do two things.

b. They, too, sing.

c. They sing in their deeper voices.

d. Another thing they do is use their dance rattles.

e. Their rattles are made from dry cocoons.

f. The cocoons are strung together with sinew cords.

g. Their dance rattles are tied to their legs.

h. Their dance rattles add a sharp, high clatter.

i. The high clatter is like the sound of shaken gourds.

j. The rattling sound is very well timed.

k. The timing is the result of the men's accurate steps.

Word Count: forty-nine (long sentence)

4a. A Bushman dance is a pattern.

b. The pattern is infinitely complicated.

c. The pattern consists of two things.

d. One thing is of voices.

e. The other thing is of rhythm.

f. The pattern is an orchestra of bodies.

SENTENCE COMPOSING

g.   The pattern makes music that has two characteristics.

h.   One characteristic is that the music is infinitely varied.

i.   The other characteristic is that the music is always precise.

Word Count: twenty-five (medium sentence)

Paragraph Three

Narration of a Bull Fight from "The Undefeated" by Ernest Hemingway (five sentences)

1a.   Manuel waved his hand.

b.   Manuel was leaning against the barrera.

c.   Manuel was watching the bull.

d.   And the gypsy ran out.

e.   The gypsy was trailing his cape.

Word Count: nineteen (medium sentence)

2a.   The bull pivoted.

b.   The bull was in full gallop.

c.   The bull's head was down.

d.   The bull's tail was rising.

Word Count: sixteen (medium sentence)

3a.   The gypsy moved.

b.   The movement was in a zigzag.

c.   And as he passed, the bull caught sight of him.

d.   The bull abandoned the cape.

e.   The reason for the abandonment was to charge the man.

Word Count: twenty-four (medium sentence)

4a.   The gyp sprinted and vaulted the red fence.

b.   The red fence was of the barrera.

c.   As the gyp sprinted and vaulted, the bull struck something.

d.   The bull struck the red fence of the barrera.

e.   The bull struck it with his horns.

Word Count: nineteen (medium sentence)

5a.   He tossed into it with his horns.

b.   He tossed into it twice.

c.   He was banging into the wood.

d.   He was banging blindly.

Word Count: twelve (short sentence)

A writer is, of course, not provided with lists of sentences to combine to produce sentences for paragraphs. The starting point of writing is an intended meaning, the idea that a writer wants to convey to readers, which is given shape in appropriate sentence structures—ones that are varied, mature, and suitable to the meaning the writer intends.

PRACTICE 5

In the last Practice the sentence breaks were indicated; here, however, they are not. For each paragraph:

1. Decide how many sentences to combine into just one sentence. Do this by combining all sentences that have related content and arranging the content in the best order within your sentence.

2. Avoid monotony. Aim for variety in sentence structure. Vary the sentence lengths (short, medium, and long) as well as the sentence structures.

3. Compare your finished paragraph with those of other students and with the author's original paragraph.

The number of words and sentences contained in the author's paragraph is indicated. It is unnecessary to duplicate that number. Use it as a rough guideline. You need not stick to the order of content present in the list of sentences. Use any order that is smooth and logical.

Paragraph One

Description of a Victorian House from *The Martian Chronicles* by Ray Bradbury. (The author's paragraph has ninety-two words and four sentences.)

1. An iron deer stood.
2. It stood outside.
3. It stood upon this lawn.
4. A Victorian house stood further up on the green.
5. The house was tall.
6. The house was brown.
7. The house was quiet in the sunlight.
8. The house was all covered with scrolls and rococo.
9. The house's windows were made of blue colored glass.
10. The house's windows were made of pink colored glass.
11. The house's windows were made of yellow colored glass.
12. The house's windows were made of green colored glass.
13. Two things were upon the porch.
14. One was geraniums.

15.   The geraniums were hairy.

16.   The other was a swing.

17.   The swing was old.

18.   The swing was hooked into the porch ceiling.

19.   The swing now swung back and forth, back and forth.

20.   The swinging occurred in a little breeze.

21.   A cupola was at the summit of the house.

22.   The cupola had diamond leaded-glass windows.

23.   The cupola had a dunce-cap roof!

Paragraph Two

A Scene at Dusk from *Winesburg, Ohio* by Sherwood Anderson. (The author's paragraph has one hundred thirty-four words and five sentences.)

1.   A man walked up and down.

2.   He was little.

3.   He was fat.

4.   He walked nervously.

5.   He walked upon the veranda.

6.   The veranda was half decayed.

7.   The veranda was of a small frame house.

8.   The house stood near the edge of a ravine.

9.   The ravine was near the town of Winesburg, Ohio.

10.   The man could see the public highway.

11.   He could see the highway across a long field.

12.   The field had been seeded for clover.

13.   The field, however, had produced only a dense crop of weeds.

14.   The weeds were yellow mustard weeds.

15.   A wagon went along the public highway.

16.   The wagon was filled with berry pickers.

17.   The berry pickers were returning from the fields.

18.   The berry pickers were youths.

19.   The berry pickers were maidens.

20.   The berry pickers laughed.

21.   The berry pickers shouted.

22.   The shouting was boisterous.

23.   A boy leaped from the wagon.

24.   The boy was clad in a shirt.

25.   The shirt was blue.

26.   The boy attempted to drag after him one of the maidens.

27.   The maiden screamed.

28.   The maiden protested.

29.   The protesting was shrill.

30.   The feet of the boy in the road kicked up a cloud.

31.   The cloud was of dust.

32.   The dust cloud floated across the face of the sun.

33.   The sun was departing.

Paragraph Three

A Hunting Accident from "The Interlopers" by Saki (The author's paragraph has one hundred sixty words and five sentences.)

1.   Ulrich von Gradwitz found himself stretched on the ground.

2.   One arm was beneath him.

3.   It was numb.

4.   The other was held almost as helplessly.

5.   This arm was held in a tight tangle of forked branches.

6.   Both legs were pinned beneath the fallen mass.

7.   His heavy shooting boots had saved his feet.

8.   The boots had saved the feet from being crushed to pieces.

9.   His fractures were not as serious as they might have been.

10.   It was evident, however, that he could not move.

11.   He could not move from his present position.

12.   He could not move from there till someone came to release him.

13.   The descending twigs had slashed the skin.

14.   The skin was of his face.

15.   He had to wink away some drops of blood from his eyelids.

16.   He had to do this before he could take in a general view.

17.   The general view was of the disaster.

18.   Someone lay at his side.

19.   The someone was so near.

20.   Under normal circumstances he could almost have touched him.

21.   Georg Znaeym was that someone.

22.   Georg was alive.

23. Georg was struggling.
24. Georg was obviously, however, as helplessly pinioned down as himself.
25. All round them lay wreckage.
26. The wreckage was thick-strewn.
27. The wreckage was of splintered branches.
28. The wreckage was of broken twigs.

Part of the writing of professional writers consists of rewriting, often many times. Many students neglect the revision stage, assuming that once the first draft is written, no changes are possible. To assume this is a mistake. One of the easiest yet most productive revision techniques available to student writers is sentence combining.

PRACTICE 6

Below are two paragraphs a student might have written as first drafts. Although the meaning in each is clear, the sentence structure could easily be improved in second drafts through sentence combining.

Paragraph One

(1) The weather report the night before mentioned the possibility of four to six inches of snow. (2) The snow was supposed to start either during the night or early the next morning. (3) I fell asleep and hoped that school would be cancelled. (4) School was usually cancelled when it snowed that much. (5) I awoke the next morning. (6) The sky was very cloudy, but there was no snow, not even a flake. (7) Reluctantly I got dressed. (8) I then ate breakfast. (9) I got in my car and drove toward school. (10) Just before I got there, the snow started. (11) When I entered school, everyone was talking about whether we would be let out of school because of the snow. (12) Nobody was very enthused about being in school that morning. (13) The students weren't. (14) The teachers weren't either. (15) The principal was standing in the cafeteria looking out the window. (16) He wasn't either. (17) The snow continued coming down heavily for about two more hours. (18) Finally, during social studies class, the principal came on the intercom. (19) He announced that school would close early because of the snow. (20) We were dismissed about twenty minutes later.

Paragraph Two

(1) I was very nervous before my driving test. (2) I had a hard time sleeping the night before. (3) I kept going over the answers to the questions

in the little driver's manual they had given me to study from. (4) I was still nervous in the test room at the Department of Motor Vehicles. (5) There were about twenty others there to take their tests. (6) Most were young, about my age. (7) There was one man who looked almost sixty. (8) He had on glasses that were the thickest I had ever seen. (9) When he spoke to ask one of the clerks where the rest room was, I noticed his foreign accent. (10) He probably knew how to drive. (11) He probably had learned in his native country. (12) He had to take the test here though to get a license in our country. (13) A middle-age woman, who was well dressed, sat two desks down from me. (14) She added to my nervousness. (15) She was talking to a girl next to her. (16) She told the girl that this part of the examination was easy. (17) She meant the written test part, not the driving part. (18) She told the girl that she had taken the drivers' examination four times. (19) Each time she had passed the written part, but not the driving part. (20) She had never passed the driving part. (21) Once she had an accident. (22) She backed into the parked car owned by the commissioner of motor vehicles. (23) Another time she jumped a curb. (24) Another time she took too long to parallel park. (25) And another time she got so tense that she started crying and could not continue.

PRACTICE 7

Choose a recent piece of your writing and combine sentences for improved economy of word usage and variety in sentence structure.

REVIEWING AND APPLYING SENTENCE COMBINING

PRACTICE 8

Combine the sentences in the following lists in one or several ways. Then compare each of yours with each original in the References. Punctuate correctly.

List of Sentences

1. One day when I went out to my woodpile, something happened.
2. Rather my pile of stumps is what I should call the woodpile.
3. What happened was that I observed two ants.
4. They were both large.
5. One was red.
6. The other was the much larger of the two ants.
7. This one was nearly half an inch long.

8.   This one was black.

9.   The ants were fiercely contending with one another.

Possible Combinations

A.   When I went out to my woodpile one day, really my pile of stumps, I observed two large ants, one red, the other black and the larger of the two, almost half an inch long, both fiercely contending with one another.

B.   Two large ants, a red one and a larger black one nearly half an inch long, were fiercely contending with one another one day when I went out to my woodpile, or rather my pile of stumps.

C.   There were two large ants, a red one and a larger black one about a half inch long, which I observed one day when I went out to my woodpile, or rather my pile of stumps; they were fiercely contending with one another.

All of the combinations work. Notice that the first follows the order of the list of sentences; the other two deviate from that order. Either procedure is acceptable if the result is a smooth sentence with mature structure. The third version is an acceptable English sentence, but in this Practice try not to depend on coordinating conjunctions or semicolons to make combinations.

Original Sentence

One day when I went out to my woodpile, or rather my pile of stumps, I observed two large ants, the one red, the other much larger, nearly half an inch long, and black, fiercely contending with one another.

Henry David Thoreau, Walden

Discuss the differences between Thoreau's sentence and the other versions. Is his better than the others? Explain.

In this Practice, aim for economy. The number of words in the author's sentence is indicated. Don't worry about using that exact number, but try not to exceed it by much.

1a.   Now the sky was without a cloud.

b.   It was pale blue.

c.   It was delicate.

d.   It was luminous.

e.   It was scintillating with morning.

Word Count: fourteen

Frank Norris, The Octopus

2a.   He distributed handbills for merchants.

b.   He did this, and the following activities, from ages ten to fifteen.

c. He held horses.

d. He ran confidential errands.

Word Count: fifteen

Thornton Wilder, The Bridge of San Luis Rey

3a. Nick looked down into the water.

b. The water was clear.

c. The water was brown.

d. The brown color came from the pebbly bottom.

e. As Nick looked down he watched the trout.

f. The trout were keeping themselves steady in the current.

g. They kept themselves steady with their fins.

h. Their fins were wavering.

Word Count: twenty-five

Ernest Hemingway, "Big Two-Hearted River"

4a. On one side was a tiny meadow.

b. The meadow began at the very lip of the pool.

c. The meadow had a surface of green.

d. The surface was cool.

e. The surface was resilient.

f. The surface extended.

g. The surface extended to the base.

h. The base was of the browning wall.

Word Count: thirty

Jack London, "All Gold Canyon"

5a. In the stillness of the air many things in the forest seemed to have been bewitched.

b. They were bewitched into an immobility.

c. The immobility was perfect.

d. The immobility was final.

e. Every tree seemed thus bewitched.

f. Every leaf seemed thus bewitched.

g. Every bough seemed thus bewitched.

h. Every tendril of creeper seemed thus bewitched.

i. Every petal of minute blossoms seemed thus bewitched.

Word Count: thirty-three

Joseph Conrad, "The Lagoon" from Tales of Unrest

6a. Let every nation know something.

b. Well-wishing nations should know it.

c. Ill-wishing nations should also.

d. All nations should know that we shall do several things.
e. We shall pay any price.
f. We shall bear any burden.
g. We shall meet any hardship.
h. We shall support any friend.
i. We shall oppose any foe.
j. We shall do all of this for two reasons.
k. We want to assure the survival of liberty.
l. We want to assure the success of liberty.

Word Count: thirty-nine

John F. Kennedy, "Inaugural Address"

7a. The mill blew its whistle.
b. The whistling happened four times a day.
c. The shrill wheeze of the saws at the mill had become a part of something.
d. The wheeze had become part of the habitual silence.
e. The whistle had two purposes.
f. One was to announce for the hands to begin work.
g. The other purpose was to announce for the hands to leave off work.
h. The sound of the whistle occurred in blasts.
i. The blasts seemed to shatter themselves.
j. The shattering occurred against the thin air.

Word Count: forty-two

William Dean Howells, *A Modern Instance*

PRACTICE 9

Write five sentences, all beginning with the same subject. Combine the sentences three times to produce three sentences, similar in content, dissimilar in sentence structure. Indicate which of the three you consider the best. Defend your choice.

List of Sentences

1. High fidelity recording was once primitive compared to today.
2. High fidelity recording began as monaural sound.
3. High fidelity recording added the illusion of a third dimension through stereophonic sound.
4. High fidelity recording is now possible in four channels, called quadraphonic sound.

5. High fidelity recording today almost duplicates the sound of a live performance.

Possible Combinations

A.   Once primitive compared to today, high fidelity recording, which began as monaural sound, added the illusion of a third dimension, and more recently became available in four channel, quadraphonic sound, almost duplicating the sound of a live performance.

B.   High fidelity recording, once primitive compared to today, began as monaural sound, then added the illusion of a third dimension through stereophonic sound, and now is possible in four channels, called quadraphonic sound, which almost duplicates the sound of a live performance.

C.   Although today almost duplicating the sound of a live performance, high fidelity recording was once primitive compared to today, having begun as monaural sound, then adding the illusion of a third dimension through stereophonic sound, and finally evolving into four channel, quadraphonic sound.

PRACTICE 10

Here is a list of twenty sentences. Following the list is a discussion of the process one writer used to group related sentences, combining those sentences to produce a paragraph characterized by mature sentence structure and logical development of the description in the paragraph.

1. Marilyn Monroe was a rare and, in her case, tragic combination of innocent little girl and experienced woman.
2. Her desire to be protected was child-like.
3. Her playfulness and giggling could either amuse or irritate people.
4. Her personal and professional insecurity made her afraid of responsibility.
5. The blonde beauty of Marilyn Monroe is legendary.
6. She was one of a series of blonde sex symbols before her like Jean Harlow and Betty Grable.
7. She resented being thought of as a sex symbol.
8. She, nevertheless, worked hard to create that identity.
9. Her acting ability has been damned as well as praised.
10. Many people and critics dismissed her as a mindless woman without acting talent.
11. Many others, however, saw her as an uneducated but very intelligent and talented actress.

12.   She suffered from a confused identity.

13.   Sometimes she thought she was loved for herself.

14.   Sometimes she thought she was loved for her public image.

15.   When she entered middle age, she felt helpless, desperate, and afraid.

16.   She used drugs to alter her moods.

17.   She had married older men who would be her protectors.

18.   She had been institutionalized several times for psychiatric problems.

19.   She imagined rejection by Hollywood and the world.

20.   She committed suicide, to the regret of Hollywood, to the shock of the world, and has only now become appreciated for her humanity, intelligence, talent, and, of course, her beauty.

Sentence One (Combination of Sentences #1, 5, 6)

Combining in one sentence comments about Monroe's physical beauty and dual personality makes a good opening for the paragraph. On your own paper, try several combinations of Sentences #1, 5, and 6 and select the combination you consider best. Use the result as the starter sentence for your paragraph.

Sentence Two (Combination of Sentences #3, 4, 2)

These three sentences refer to Monroe's childlike behavior and its differing effects on people. Try several combinations of Sentences #3, 4, and 2 and select the combination you consider best. Add it to the paragraph you began above.

Sentence Three (Combination of Sentences #12, 13, 14, 7, 8)

In these sentences a lot of content is grouped for use in just one sentence, a total of five sentences to be combined into one. Even though the resulting sentence will be long, if it is well-structured, it will be a good one, unified around the topic of Monroe's confused identity. Try several combinations of Sentences #12, 13, 14, 7, and 8 and select the combination you consider best. Add it to your paragraph.

Sentence Four (Combination of Sentences #9, 10, 11)

These sentences extend the topic begun in the last sentence—her confused identity. Whereas the unity in Sentence Three was based on the confusion surrounding her personal life, in Sentence Four it is based on the confusion surrounding her professional life as an actress. Try several combinations of Sentences #9, 10, and 11 and select the combination you consider best. Add it to your paragraph.

Sentence Five (Combination of Sentences #15, 17, 18, 16, 19, 20)

With six sentences to combine into one, the resulting sentence, the last one in the paragraph, will be the longest. It will deal with the contributing factors that led to her untimely death and the effects it had on the world. Notice the order in which the sentences are listed. Sentence Five will begin by setting a time period (middle-age, Sentence #15) and an assessment of her mood then (depressed, Sentence #15). It will next trace the development of her depression, beginning with two past factors (many marriages, Sentence #17, and frequent institutionalization, Sentence #18). Next are more recent factors (drug use, Sentence #16, and sense of rejection, Sentence #19). Finally, the sentence ends with the unfortunate result (suicide, Sentence #20) and the reaction of people (reassessment of Marilyn Monroe, Sentence #20). Try several combinations of Sentences #15, 17, 18, 16, 19, and 20 and select the combination you consider best. Add it as the final sentence of your paragraph.

After you have completed your work on the paragraph, compare your result with that of another writer who produced a paragraph based on the same sentences. Find that paragraph in the References.

PRACTICE 11

Produce a paragraph on the story of Noah. Group the related sentences listed below and then combine them. Your finished paragraph should have no more than ten sentences.

1. God didn't like the behavior of men.
2. He thought it was evil.
3. He was sorry He had created man.
4. He decided to destroy all of creation, especially human beings.
5. There was an exception.
6. The exception was a good man, one of few.
7. The man's name was Noah.
8. He told Noah to build an ark.
9. He told him to gather two of every species, male and female sex, to go with him on the ark.
10. Noah took his wife, his three sons, and their wives.
11. God caused it to rain for forty days and forty nights.
12. During this time, Noah and the others were sailing in the ark.
13. They were spared death.
14. Everything else in creation was covered with the flood waters.
15. All animal, vegetable, and mineral life was destroyed.

16. Eventually the flood waters receded.

17. Noah sent a dove to see if the dove could find dry land.

18. If the dove did, that would tell Noah to look for a shore and to return to dry land.

19. The dove flew back to Noah and the others on the ark.

20. The dove held in its beak an olive branch.

21. This was good news for Noah and the others.

22. This branch is a symbol.

23. It symbolizes peace, as does the dove.

24. The story ends with God's promise to Noah.

25. He promises never again to destroy creation by water.

26. He sends forth a rainbow to symbolize his promise.

27. The promise is the basis for a new covenant with people.

28. God will give people another chance to follow Him and to obey His commandments.

29. Noah, in a way, was like a second Adam.

30. Like Adam, he became the head of the human race, with millions of people descending from him.

PRACTICE 12

Using twenty short sentences, describe a person: a friend, a teacher, a relative, or someone from sports, literature, television, or history. Without changing the content of the sentences (although you might want to make changes in the wording), combine them into a paragraph of from five to ten sentences. Try several combinations of related groups of sentences. Don't settle for your first attempt. Choose only the one combination you consider your best and add it to your paragraph.

PRACTICE 13

Select two paragraphs, each at least ten sentences in length, from a piece of writing you have recently done. The paragraphs may be from the same piece of writing or from two different ones. For each paragraph, using sentence combining, reduce the ten sentences to seven or fewer. In the revised sentences aim for variety of sentence structure and sentence length.

Sentence combining is an easy, effective revision technique. You should use it regularly.

4
Sentence Expanding

DEFINING SENTENCE EXPANDING

Sentence expanding is a process for changing minimal sentences into sentences like those of professional writers: maximal sentences. It transforms underdeveloped sentences into fully developed sentences.

One important contrast in the way professional writers and students compose sentences is that the professional, aware of the great potential for variations within just one sentence, frequently provides a much greater amount of content per sentence. In short, professionals get more sentence mileage. There are several reasons for this. One is that they have had more practice in interrelating content within just one sentence and are more familiar with how to structure and organize the sentence parts within their sentences. Also, because they usually write with the purpose of expression of self rather than in compliance with *someone else's purposes*—a composition assignment that is required for history, for example—their motivation is stronger. Students sometimes "stretch" content simply to meet the minimum length requirement for writing assignments.

Given the same content to be communicated, a professional writer and a student writer would probably express that content differently: the writer, more concisely, with fewer sentences, but with each sentence packed, and with sentence structure that clearly shows the interrelationships among the various parts of the sentence.

Reduced Sentence

There stood two squat old-fashioned decanters of cut glass.

Expanded Sentence

In the centre of the table **there stood,** as sentries to a fruit-stand which upheld a pyramid of oranges and American apples, **two squat old-fashioned decanters of cut glass,** one containing port and the other dark sherry.

James Joyce, "The Dead"

Added are three sentence parts (expansions) in the expanded sentence: one at the beginning *(In the centre of the table),* which tells the exact location of the decanters; one in the middle separating the subject and verb *(as sentries to a fruit-stand which upheld a pyramid of oranges and American apples),* which identifies the impression the decanters give *(sentries to a fruit-stand)* and describes the fruit-stand; and one at the end *(one containing port and the other dark sherry),* which describes the contents of the two decanters. The content of the reduced sentence is detailed through the additions of these three sentence parts; the structure of the sentence is more mature, varied, and professional.

Sentence expanding improves both content and structure. Joyce could have written the same content in more than one sentence. Compare this version, a rewrite of the original, with Joyce's original sentence:

Two squat old-fashioned decanters stood there. They were in the centre of the table. They were like sentries to a fruit-stand near them. The fruit-stand upheld a pyramid of oranges and American apples. One of the decanters contained port. The other one contained sherry.

The rewrite is poorer than the original one-sentence version for several reasons. It is uneconomical, using six sentences to express what Joyce did in just one sentence; it uses forty-seven words to Joyce's thirty-nine. It is poorly organized, failing to show as clearly as Joyce's the interrelationships among the various objects described. It is uninteresting, beginning each of the six sentences in the same monotonous way, with the subject immediately followed by a verb.

Subject	*Verb*
1. decanters	stood
2. they	were
3. they	were
4. fruit-stand	upheld
5. one	contained
6. one	contained

Length, by itself, does not determine whether a sentence is effective. A long sentence can be ineffective; a short one, effective; and vice-versa. Don't think that professional writers use only long, highly expanded sentences. They don't. What characterizes their sentences is the skillful interaction among the sentences in their paragraphs—some short, some medium, others long, some expanded, and the rest unexpanded. Yet regardless of length or degree of expansion, they are all effective.

PRACTICE 1

Study the sentences in the paragraphs that open the novel *Bless the Beasts and Children* by Glendon Swarthout. Count the number of short sentences (one to fifteen words), medium sentences (sixteen to thirty), and long sentences (thirty-one and above). Count the number of expanded sentences. (The main expansions within sentences are in boldface.) Discuss the reasons why the author expanded some sentences but not others, citing specific sentences as examples.

1. Cotton dreamed.

2. Six of them waited in early morning, **held in a kind of enclosure behind thick posts and planks and bunched up not because they were afraid but because, unused to being penned, they were excited and, close together, they could communicate by odor.** 3. They snuffed one another. 4. Through dilated nostrils they drew in the hot, animal odor of their excitement.

5. Then men came, **horsemen.** 6. A gate was opened. 7. **Shouted at,** they tried to stampede out together, but the gate was slammed after the lead three, **Teft and Shecker and Lally 1,** were through. 8. The others waited. 9. Soon the air was split by riflefire. 10. It spooked the three remaining. 11. They milled in circles, **bending planks and sideswiping posts, unafraid yet more excited than ever, since it was a stimulus in the ear which they could not identify.** 12. In the after-silence they waited again.

13. The horsemen returned. 14. The gate was opened, and the last three, **Cotton and Goodenow and Lally 2,** were let out down a lane of wire fencing. 15. It was good to be unpenned and free in the vivid morning. 16. **But when they paused to drink from a pond,** the horsemen harried them on, **waving hats and shouting.**

17. In an open field they made a stand. 18. One hundred yards away a line of vehicles confronted them, and **before the vehicles,** a line of humans. 19. **Released earlier,** Teft and Shecker and Lally 1 were nowhere to be seen. 20. This puzzled them, **as did the gunshot and Goodenow's going down, first to his knees, then folding his hindquarters, then heavily upon one side.** 21. He did not move. 22. Cotton and Lally 2 snuffed the new strange odor emanating from the carcass.

23. At the next report Lally 2 leaped up and came down stifflegged, and as the other violences in the ear shook his head and toppled, **his eyes glazed, his limbs doubling and extending convulsively and brilliant red blowing from his mouth and nose.** 24. Cotton snuffed the blood. 25. This smell he knew.

26. One lunge sent him into top speed, **running this way only to be turned by vehicles, running that way only to be hemmed in by horsemen.** 27. **Snorting,**

he tried another, **battering head down into a wire fence and recoiling upon his haunches.** 28. He bounded up, **maddened by the obstacle of steel which must give way before him.**

29. **Raging,** he stood. 30. **Omnipotent, glaring at the line of humans,** he centered on the muzzle of a rifle and down the barrel and into the half-face of a woman seated on a tarpaulin sighting him. 31. She fired. 32. He recognized her. 33. The microsecond's recognition shattered his heart even as her bullet broke his brain. 34. It was the face of his mother.

35. Cotton woke with a cry.

36. His forehead, palms, and inner thighs seeped sweat. 37. He disgusted himself. 38. He was fifteen, **the oldest, too old to have bad dreams.**

All of these sentences—short or long, expanded or unexpanded—are effective, vividly descriptive, with strong interaction within the paragraphs that contain them.

The Practices in this section on sentence expanding will teach you how to expand sentences, but you should not conclude that you are being encouraged to expand every sentence you write. *When to expand, and when not to expand,* is a skill that can be acquired by paying attention to the practice of professional writers. *How to expand* is a skill you can learn by doing the Practices in this part of the book.

The following Practice illustrates the difference between a reduced sentence and an expanded sentence. The first sentence in each pair is the reduced version—"bare bones" content, "lean" sentence structure. The next sentence in each pair is the original, an expanded sentence that includes the reduced sentence plus added structures to create a maximal sentence. The sentence parts that make up the expansion are placed where their content and structure will blend smoothly with the reduced sentence.

PRACTICE 2

Compare the reduced sentence and the expanded sentence in each pair, noting the quantity, position, and length of each expansion. Write an imitation retaining the complete reduced sentence (content and structure) but retaining only the *structure* of the expansions that were added while providing new content. The new content should blend smoothly with the retained content and structure of the reduced sentence.

Reduced Sentence

There stood two squat old-fashioned decanters of cut glass.

Expanded Sentence

In the centre of the table **there stood,** as sentries to a fruit-stand which upheld a pyramid of oranges and American apples, **two squat old-fashioned decanters of cut glass,** one containing port and the other dark sherry.

James Joyce, "The Dead"

Imitation

On a shelf in the china closet **there stood,** like fragile sculptures which boasted an old age and genteel birth, **two squat old-fashioned decanters of cut glass,** one opened, the other unopened.

1a. Smog can now be found all over the country.

b. Smog, **which was once the big attraction of Los Angeles,** can now be found all over the country, **from Butte, Montana to New York City ...**

Art Buchwald, "Fresh Air Will Kill You"

2a. With them was Elmo Goodhue Pipgrass.

b. With them, **carrying a gnarled walking stick,** was Elmo Goodhue Pipgrass, **the littlest, oldest man I had ever seen.**

Max Shulman, "The Unlucky Winner"

3a. I chewed thoughtfully on a peanut-butter-and-jelly sandwich, while my mother droned on monotonously.

b. **Later that night, hunched over the kitchen table, still somewhat numbed by the unexpected turn of events,** I chewed thoughtfully on a peanut-butter-and-jelly sandwich, while my mother, **hanging over the sink in her rump-sprung Chinese-red chenille bathrobe,** droned on monotonously ....

Jean Shepherd, "Wanda Hickey's Night of Golden Memories"

4a. It was shown that Buck Fanshaw had taken arsenic, shot himself through the body, cut his throat, and jumped out of a four-story window and broken his neck—and the jury brought in a verdict of death "by the visitation of God."

b. **On the inquest** it was shown that Buck Fanshaw, **in the delirium of a wasting typhoid fever,** had taken arsenic, shot himself through the body, cut his throat, and jumped out of a four-story window and broken his neck—and **after due deliberation,** the jury, **sad and tearful, but with intelligence unblinded by its sorrow,** brought in a verdict of death "by the visitation of God."

Mark Twain, "Buck Fanshaw's Funeral"

It's important to remember that many different types of structures could have been used in the places where the expansions occur. Realizing the great variety that is possible allows a writer to have a freedom of choice, selecting from the many the most effective one.

Reduced Sentence

The kid was a boy of ten.

Author's Expansion

The kid was a boy of ten, **with bas-relief freckles, and hair the color of the cover of the magazine you buy at the newsstand when you want to catch a train.**

O. Henry, "The Ransom of Red Chief"

A. Expanding in Same Position

Using a Different Structure

The kid was a boy of ten **who never told a lie, never did not eat everything on his plate, almost never refused to go to bed at his parents' request, always complying, obeying them in a way that some thought excessive, unnatural, a little bit scary.**

Using a Different Length (Either Shorter or Longer)

The kid was a boy of ten, **the block bully, his voice more of a weapon than his muscles.**

B. Expanding in Different Position(s)

Faster than anyone else on the team, most of whom had trained all summer, the kid was a boy of ten.

The kid, **who spoke Spanish and English and could read German and Swedish,** was a boy of ten.

PRACTICE 3

Expand the first four reduced sentences in the same positions as the author's expansions but use new structures. Expand the next four in the same positions as the author's expansions but use different lengths (shorter or longer). Expand the next four in different positions from the author's expansions—at least one expansion per reduced sentence. Use original content for all the expansions. See above for examples.

In all twelve expansions be certain that the content and structure blend smoothly with the content and structure of the reduced sentence.

Expand in Same Position Using New Structures

1a. They had grown up next door to each other.

  b. They had grown up next door to each other, **on the fringe of a city, near** fields and woods and orchards, within sight of a lovely bell tower that belonged to a school for the blind.

Kurt Vonnegut, Jr., Welcome to the Monkey House

2a. Tarzan of the Apes sidled nearer and nearer.

b. **Stooped, his muscles rigid and one great shoulder turned toward the young bull,** Tarzan of the Apes sidled nearer and nearer.

Edgar Rice Burroughs, "Tarzan's First Love"

3a. He forgot them.

b. **As soon as the talking ceased and the women left,** he forgot them.

Willa Cather, Youth and the Bright Medusa

4a. His clothes and his manner seemed to indicate that he might be better placed than she had imagined.

b. His clothes and his manner, **as well as a remark he had dropped, to the effect that he was connected with the company in some official capacity,** seemed to indicate that he might be better placed than she had imagined.

Theodore Dreiser, An American Tragedy

Expand in Same Position Using Shorter Length

5a. David had been in his old room a few blocks from the University, waiting.

b. **About seven years before that day, in early October,** David had been in his old room a few blocks from the University, waiting.

Joyce Carol Oates, The Wheel of Love and Other Stories

6a. He adjusted a pleasant little cap of bright scarlet.

b. **On his head, which had been skillfully deprived of every scrap of hair,** he adjusted a pleasant little cap of bright scarlet, **held on by suction and inflated with hydrogen, and curiously like the comb of a cock.**

H. G. Wells, "A Cure for Love"

Expand in Same Position Using Longer Length

7a. Aggie flew down and sat on his dictionary.

b. Aggie, **his favorite,** flew down and sat on his dictionary.

Laurie Colwin, "Animal Behavior"

8a. About seven years before that day, in early October, David had been in his old room a few blocks from the University.

b. About seven years before that day, in early October, David had been in his old room a few blocks from the University, **waiting.**

Joyce Carol Oates, The Wheel of Love and Other Stories

Expand in Different Positions

Slash marks are used to indicate the position for *new,* added expansions. Add commas where necessary.

9a. I could see the flashlights of the policemen as they quartered the hillside.

b. I could see the flashlights of the policemen as they quartered the hillside, hunting for their murderer.

Leonard Wolf, "Fifty-Fifty"

c. /I could see the flashlights of the policemen / as they quartered the hillside, hunting for their murderer.

10a. Ashurst squeezed the hand.

b. Stirred and moved, Ashurst squeezed the hand, and went downstairs.

John Galsworthy, *Five Tales*

c. / stirred and moved, Ashurst squeezed the hand / and went downstairs.

11a. She spread her arms and stood there swan-like.

b. Slowly, she spread her arms and stood there swan-like, radiating a pride in her young perfection that lit a warm glow in Carlyle's heart.

F. Scott Fitzgerald, *Flappers and Philosophers*

c. / slowly, she spread her arms / and stood there swan-like, radiating a pride in her young perfection that lit a warm glow in Carlyle's heart /.

12a. He got into the shower.

b. He got into the shower, put on fresh clothes, and felt a little easier.

William Saroyan, "Boys and Girls Together"

c. / he got into the shower /, put on fresh clothes /, and felt a little easier / .

PRACTICING SENTENCE EXPANDING

In order to use sentence expanding in your own writing, you must be aware of the expansion possibilities in any sentence—possibilities for "telling more" about the people, places, things, manners, actions, incidents, opinions, explanations, and descriptions mentioned.

Are there any limits to sentence expanding? Is there a point where an expanded sentence, like a balloon filled to over-capacity, could "burst"? The answer to this question is that as long as a sentence is clear in meaning, it is not over-expanded, regardless of how many words are in the sentence, regardless of how many different structures are present, regardless of how many ideas are packed into it. Among American writers, William Faulkner is famous for the ultralong sentences that characterize his style. The French writer Victor Hugo is often cited as having written one of the longest sentences ever, one that has hundreds of words, in *Les Miserables*. The Irish writer James Joyce went even further, ending his novel *Ulysses* with a sentence that runs over twenty pages!

Even among professional writers, however, such ultralong sentences are rare. Still, on the average, sentences by professional writers are longer than those by students. Sentence expanding practice will make you more aware of the potential for revising your sentences so that they're more like those of the experts.

PRACTICE 4

For the first four reduced sentences, add one expansion, deciding where to expand and what structure and length to use. Then compare yours with the originals in the References. (The original sentences have just one expansion.) Punctuate correctly. For the next four reduced sentences, add two expansions, deciding where to expand and what structure and length to use. Then compare yours to the originals in the References. (The original sentences have two expansions.) Punctuate correctly.

Add One Expansion

1.   In the hall stood an enormous trunk.
From a sentence by Willa Cather, *Youth and the Bright Medusa*

2.   All members of the staff wore plastic tags bearing their names and color photographs.
From a sentence by Laurie Colwin, "Animal Behavior"

3.   Jerry stood on the landing.
From a sentence by Joyce Carol Oates, *The Wheel of Love and Other Stories*

4.   They lived in a square two-flat house tightly packed among identical houses in a fog-enveloped street in the Sunset district of San Francisco.
From a sentence by William Saroyan, "Boys and Girls Together"

Add Two Expansions

5.   His teeth were pitifully inadequate by comparison with the mighty fighting fangs of the anthropoids.
From a sentence by Edgar Rice Burroughs, "Tarzan's First Love"

6.   He used to ride, alone.
From a sentence by Nancy Hale, "The Rider Was Lost"

7.   She tossed her book to the deck and hurried to the rail.
From a sentence by F. Scott Fitzgerald, *Flappers and Philosophers*

8.   It is hardly surprising that so many people lose their tempers with so many other people.
From a sentence by Shirley Jackson, "About Two Nice People"

PRACTICE 5

Below is a list of reduced sentences, each short and grammatically correct but typical of sentences written by children first learning to write. For each reduced sentence, create four sentences, each retaining the reduced sentence and expanding it in four different ways.

Reduced Sentence

The old man smiled.

Four Different Sentence Expansions

1.   **Now content that he would be able to stay in the place he loved, the home he had lived in since he and Jennifer had started their family so many years ago,** the old man smiled.

2.   The old man smiled **because the insurance agent did in fact think that the man's robustness, his spirit, his incredible overall health made his immortality almost certain.**

3.   The old man, **remembering the park on Sundays where he took the children to see the balloon man and buy hot roasted peanuts,** smiled.

4.   **Pulling on his gloves and throwing the scarf around his neck,** the old man, **his complexion shining and pink like the skin of a young girl,** smiled, **blinking knowingly at Bob, sharing with him his warmth, his understanding, his good humor.**

In these examples, the expansion occurs at the beginning of the reduced sentence (#1), in the middle (#3), at the end (#2), and in all three places (#4).

In expanding the reduced sentences below, vary the position of your expansions and aim for variety in structure and content.

1.   The child cried.
2.   The President listened.
3.   The teacher frowned.
4.   The mailman ran.
5.   The runner stumbled.

Often, in actually composing sentences, what the writer has in mind while writing is a small part of the sentence—a phrase or a clause—and not the complete sentence. That comes in the act of writing—the writer, in a sense, discovers what he or she wants to say in the process of saying it.

PRACTICE 6

Below is a list of phrases that might be considered "sentence starters." This list, unlike the list of the last Practice, is made up of only sentence parts, phrases that are not grammatically complete sentences. (The last Practice listed grammatically complete sentences—although they were hardly mature sentences.)

Expand each sentence starter below to produce four different sentences. Vary the structure and content. Vary the position of the sentence starter, sometimes placing it at the beginning, sometimes after the beginning, and sometimes near the end.

Sentence Starter

picking up the soggy newspaper

Four Different Sentence Expansions

1.   Picking up the soggy newspaper, **which had been hidden there by the now-melted snow, she shook it to remove any loose water and furiously turned its pages to see if the story had made the papers.**

2.   Picking up the soggy newspaper, **a victim of Tim's over-enthusiastic watering of the lawn, he shouted to Tim to get his aim right, quit clowning, or he'd come after him.**

3.   **When his aim proved inaccurate, he got out of the car and,** picking up the soggy newspaper, **tossed it again, this time with better aim.**

4.   **The dog,** picking up the soggy newspaper, **tramped over to Gramps, snoozing soundly for his noontime nap, dropped it squarely in his lap, took its paw and manhandled poor Gramps to awakening, badgering the old guy for the reward.**

Sentence Starters

1.   when the alarm went off
2.   his legs aching with pain
3.   near the old ruin of a house children thought haunted
4.   getting up the nerve to finally ask (him/her) out
5.   blinking from the intense light, trying to shut off the ears from the stabbing sound

PRACTICE 7

Compare your sentence expansions with those of professional writers. A slash mark indicates a place where the professional writer expanded the reduced sentence. The number indicates how many words were used in each expansion. Expand each reduced sentence in the place indicated by the slash mark, using approximately the same number of words. Compare yours with the author's in the References. Punctuate correctly.

Reduced Sentences

1.   She sprang dynamically to her feet, /3, then swiftly and noiselessly crossed over to her bed and, /3, dragged out her suitcase.
F. Scott Fitzgerald, "Bernice Bobs Her Hair"

2.   He stood there, /4, and Rainsford, /6, heard the general's mocking laugh ring through the jungle.
Richard Connell, "The Most Dangerous Game"

3.   /4 he knocked the big man down, and the big man came again, /9.
Maurice Walsh, "The Quiet Man"

4.   We spent several evenings together, and the last one was the funniest, /15.
Bennett Cerf, At Random

5.   That night in the south upstairs chamber, /18, Emmett lay in a kind of trance.
Jessamyn West, "A Time of Learning"

6.   /21, Paul dressed and dashed whistling down the corridor to the elevator.
Willa Cather, "Paul's Case"

7.   Adolph Knipe took a sip of stout, /41.
Roald Dahl, "The Great Automatic Grammatisator"

PRACTICE 8

In the last Practice you were given reduced sentences to expand. Now try expanding sentence parts and compare your expansion with those in the References.

The slash marks indicate the places for expansions. The number shows how many words were used by the professional writer, but do not be restricted by it. Use it only as a general guideline for the length of the expansion.

Sentence Part

Absorbed in the new life he was entering upon, intoxicated with the sparkle, the ripple, the scents and the sounds and the sunlight, /12.
From a sentence by Kenneth Grahame, The Wind in the Willows

The above is a part of Kenneth Grahame's sentence, and, by itself, it is grammatically incomplete. To expand this sentence starter, something that includes a main clause—approximately twelve words in length—must be added to it in the place indicated by the slash mark. Here are some possible expansions. Notice that they are all different in content, different in structure, and different in number of words; but all blend smoothly with the sentence part provided, and all are grammatically correct.

Possible Expansions

1. Absorbed in the new life he was entering upon, intoxicated with the sparkle, the ripple, the scents and the sounds and the sunlight, **he started the camp fire, opened the can of beans, and sang softly to himself.**

2. Absorbed in the new life he was entering upon, intoxicated with the sparkle, the ripple, the scents and the sounds and the sunlight, **feeling alive for the first time in years, free from the dusty, fetid air of the office, he took a deep breath.**

3. Absorbed in the new life he was entering upon, intoxicated with the sparkle, the ripple, the scents and the sounds and the sunlight, **with enough hope that the mood would be continued throughout the day, and last a lifetime, he knocked on the door of the hut of the village child, his first patient.**

Original Sentence

Absorbed in the new life he was entering upon, intoxicated with the sparkle, the ripple, the scents and the sounds and the sunlight, **he trailed a paw in the water and dreamed long waking dreams.**

From a sentence by Kenneth Grahame, *The Wind in the Willows*

Expand each sentence part three times, each time with new content.

1. On the outskirts of town, /5, though at first she did not realize it.

From a sentence by Elizabeth Enright, "Nancy"

2. /7, sweet, hot, and warming in his empty stomach.

From a sentence by Ernest Hemingway, "The Undefeated"

3. When the hostess saw that I was awake and that my safety belt was already fastened, /9, waking the other passengers and asking them to fasten their safety belts.

From a sentence by Robert Bingham, "The Unpopular Passenger"

4. Running up the street with all his might, /11.

From a sentence by Murray Heyert, "The New Kid"

5. Placing a cigarette between his lips, /13.

From a sentence by Liam O'Flaherty, "The Sniper"

6. At night, untired after the day's work, /14.

From a sentence by Jessamyn West, "A Time of Learning"

7. There, in a four-roomed, lime-washed, thatched cottage, /25.

From a sentence by Maurice Walsh, "The Quiet Man"

REVIEWING AND APPLYING SENTENCE EXPANDING

There are many ways to practice expanding a sentence. One is to determine the number of expansions—one or several. Another is to expand in different sentence positions. A third is to vary the length—some short, some medium, and some long.

Varying the Number

Reduced Sentence

I made several contacts in Europe.

Expansions

Upon realizing the great demand for my product, I made several contacts in Europe. (one expansion)

Upon realizing the great demand for my product, a new process for increasing the heat that comes through thermal windows, I made several **prospective** contacts in Europe, **each with control of big markets.** (several expansions)

Varying the Position

Reduced Sentence

Kreeger will give you his version.

Expansions

Kreeger, **the witness nearest the accident,** will give you his version.

The witness nearest the accident, Kreeger will give you his version.

Varying the Length

Reduced Sentence

Glakin unrolled the blueprints.

Expansions

Glakin, **tense but assertive,** unrolled the blueprints. (short)

Glakin, **setting all of the clutter off the kitchen table to make room for them and letting everybody gather around to see,** unrolled the blueprints. (longer)

PRACTICE 9

Expand each sentence below twice. The first time, use only one expansion. The second time, with entirely new content, use at least two expansions.

1.   The mailman walked into the foyer full of people.
2.   Miss Jablonski dropped the chalk and bent to retrieve it.

3. He abruptly left his seat in the movie and stormed out.
4. He was afraid his children would turn into "videots" from TV addiction.
5. She scratched her head and turned to look out the window.

PRACTICE 10

Expand each sentence below twice. The first time, use one position. The second time, retaining the exact expansion from the first time, reposition the expansion where it will fit smoothly with the rest of the sentence.

1. Jim pulled his car to a stop.
2. The rain lasted into the night.
3. She stood and sharply criticized the plan.
4. He simply strolled across the end zone to score.
5. His fingers played the typewriter.

PRACTICE 11

Expand each sentence below twice. The first time, use a short expansion. The second time, with entirely new content, use a longer expansion.

1. The milkshake was an original creation.
2. A strong wind hurled the box.
3. Near the shopping mall was a grove of trees.
4. His mirrored reflection was startling.

PRACTICE 12

Each sentence below is a reduced version of an expanded sentence of a professional writer. You are not told the number, position, and length of the expansions. You must decide all three. After you have finished, compare your sentences with those of the professional authors in the References. Note similarities and dissimilarities in the expansions: the number, the position, and the length.

The only guideline given is the number of words in the reduced version and the number of words in the original sentence. Try to expand the reduced sentence to approximately the same length as the original. Do not add any main clauses, only phrases and subordinate clauses.

1. The chest was there. (four words, seven words)
   From a sentence by Antoine de Saint-Exupéry, *Wind, Sand, and Stars*
2. He can feel the eyes on him. (seven words, fourteen words)
   From a sentence by Judith Guest, *Ordinary People*

3.   She made the best meatloaf in the world. (eight words, twenty-four words)

From a sentence by Nancy Friday, *My Mother / My Self*

4.   Weary made Billy take a very close look at his trench knife. (twelve words, twenty-seven words)

From a sentence by Kurt Vonnegut, Jr., *Slaughter-House Five*

5.   The gardens were laid out so neatly. (seven words, twenty-eight words)

From a sentence by Judith Guest, *Ordinary People*

6.   A pale silk scarf is tied around his neck. (nine words, twenty-nine words)

From a sentence by Philip Roth, *The Professor of Desire*

7.   The four animals continued to lead their lives. (eight words, thirty words)

From a sentence by Kenneth Grahame, *The Wind in the Willows*

8.   He went into the kitchen. (five words, thirty-one words)

From a sentence by Kurt Vonnegut, Jr., *Slaughter-House Five*

Here are two versions of the same paragraph. In the first version, all of the sentences from the original paragraph have been reduced to main clauses. In the second paragraph, all of the sentences are as originally written by the author, with the reduced sentences now greatly expanded through addition of phrases and subordinate clauses.

Evaluate the differences between the two paragraphs. Contrast sentence lengths, amount of content, degree of interest for the reader, and sentence structure variety.

Version One: (Reduced Sentences)

1. A group of sailors in loincloths were quarreling on a corner. 2. Their strange voices clamored in the heat, and a knife glittered. 3. Keptah moved along. 4. Lucanus sighed. 5. There was more to life than philosophy. 6. Hot bodies pressed around his donkey, and there was an acridness of sweat everywhere. 7. Dry palms scattered themselves along the streets. 8. Peddlers shrilled their wares and ran after the boy and man on bare brown feet, and then cried curses upon them. 9. Beggars sat against walls.

Version Two: (Expansion)

1. A group of sailors in loincloths, **and with great golden rings in their ears,** were quarreling on a corner, **their blackened faces fierce and violent, their gestures vehement.** 2. Their strange voices, **speaking in a tongue Lucanus did not recognize,** clamored in the heat, and a knife glittered. 3. Keptah moved along **as if he were alone.** 4. Lucanus sighed. 5. There was more to life than philosophy. 6. Hot bodies pressed around his donkey, and there was an acridness of sweat everywhere. 7. Dry palms, **sifting with dust,** scattered

themselves along the streets. 8. Peddlers, **carrying trays of sweetmeats, blown with flies,** shrilled their wares and ran after the boy and man on bare brown feet, and then, **discomfited,** cried curses upon them. 9. Beggars sat against walls, **wailing, rattling their cups, their beards tangled and filthy.**

Taylor Caldwell, *Dear and Glorious Physician*

Notice that six out of the nine sentences are expanded. All of the expansions are phrases, except one *(as if he were alone),* which is a subordinate clause. The three sentences that are not expanded nevertheless add variety to the sentences in the paragraph through their short length, which draws attention to their content, emphasizing a key idea in the paragraph: "There was more to life than philosophy."

PRACTICE 13

In the modern horror story *Salem's Lot* by Stephen King, a vampire's death is described in vivid detail in sentences that are skillfully expanded.

Below is a version of the paragraph describing the vampire's death with the original sentences reduced to their main clauses. Provide the expansions in the places indicated by slash marks. Next to the slash mark is the number of words used by King in the original; use this number as a general guideline for the number of words to use in the expansion. Follow the indicated punctuation. Compare your paragraph with King's in the References.

Reduced Sentence

Blood splashed upward in a cold gush, /3.

Expansion

Blood splashed upward in a cold gush, **like water from a burst pipe.**

Original

Blood splashed upward in a cold gush, **blinding him momentarily.**

Paragraph of Reduced Sentences

The mouth widened gapingly /8, /12. The fingernails went black and peeled off, and then there were only bones, /4, /5. Dust puffed through the fibers of the linen shirt. The bald and wrinkled head became a skull. The pants, /6, fell away to broomsticks clad in black silk.

From a paragraph by Stephen King, *Salem's Lot*

As you compose sentences, be aware of the many positions within a sentence where expansions are possible. Here is a sentence with slash marks indicating the places for potential expansion:

/ The / diver / sprang / from the / board /.

There are six such places, although it is unlikely that any professional writer would use all six. For each of the six places for potential expansion, here are examples.

1.   **Taking a deep breath,** the diver sprang from the board. (/the)
2.   The **tall, lanky** diver sprang from the board. (The / diver)
3.   The diver, **his body taut and his mind rigidly concentrating,** sprang from the board. (diver / sprang)
4.   The diver sprang, **arching gracefully, like a ballerina,** from the board. (sprang / from)
5.   The diver sprang from the **highest, most challenging** board. (the / board)
6.   The diver sprang from the board, **his arms stretching upward for the somersault.** (board/)

In each of the six sentences, the main clause is the same *(The diver sprang from the board.)*. Each expansion includes content and structure in one of the six places for potential expansion. It is, of course, possible to include more than one expansion.

Two Expansions

Taking a deep breath, the diver, **his body taut and his mind rigidly concentrating,** sprang from the board.

More Than Two Expansions

Taking a deep breath, the diver, **his body taut and his mind rigidly concentrating,** sprang, **arching gracefully, like a ballerina,** from the **highest, most challenging** board.

PRACTICE 14

Slash marks in each of these sentences indicate places for potential expansion. Vary the length, structure, and number of expansions. Punctuate correctly.

1.   / The car / turned / the corner /.
2.   / At exactly noon / the gunfight began, and the spectators / indicated / their favorite.

3.   One of the policemen / ran through the crowd / neared the fire / and entered the smoke-filled jail /.

4.   The snowstorm / began / at dawn and continued / three days straight /.

5.   / He asked the girl in the white dress / to dance, but she / appeared to refuse his offer /.

Here is a simple paragraph describing Christmas shopping:

1. I finally decided to start my annual Christmas shopping. 2. The shopping list didn't present too much of a problem. 3. The first store was brightly decorated but crowded. 4. The little old man looked like a tiny Santa Claus dressed in a business suit. 5. I felt better when I had made my first purchase. 6. I bought a shopping bag. 7. So I finished all my shopping in just under three hours. 8. I put the brimful shopping bag on the back seat and drove home.

Each sentence in the paragraph could easily be expanded. Here is a student version with the expansions in boldface.

1. **After saving money all year, denying myself books, movies, and additions to my plant collection so that my aunt, parents, and greedy sibling could all have gifts,** I finally, **after much contemplation, conquered my fear of being trampled by raging, desperate December gift hunters and** decided to start my annual Christmas shopping. 2. **Since everything that they all wanted was either clothing or sports equipment,** the shopping list didn't present too much of a problem. 3. The first store, **a newly-built department store with smoke-colored windows,** was brightly decorated but crowded **with rows and racks of merchandise added for the Christmas shoppers: harried mothers, husbands and boyfriends who never know what to buy, girls who love to look at everything before they decide, and ostensibly benign old ladies.** 4. The little old man **who was trying to get the attention of the only saleslady in the lingerie department** looked like a tiny Santa Claus dressed in a business suit. 5. I felt better when I had made my first purchase, **a silk half-slip for my aunt that I hoped she wouldn't think impractical.** 6. **Realizing that my purchases would eventually amount to more than two arms could manage without dropping some and crushing others,** I bought a shopping bag. 7. So, **determined to be home in time to watch** *Gone With the Wind,* **running here and there for the rest of the gifts,** I finished all of my shopping in just under three hours. 8. **After rushing to my car, careful not to trip on the ice and ruin the gift wraps, when I got to the parking lot** I put the brimful shopping bag on the back seat and drove home, **finished at last and delighted to end it all with a surplus of ten dollars.**

PRACTICE 15

Place two expansions in each sentence in the paragraph below. Decide where, what kind, and how long. The quality of the final paragraph will depend on the quality of the expansions you make. Vary the placement of the expansions—some at the beginning, some in the middle, and some at the end. Underline each expansion. Punctuate correctly.

I awoke on the first day back to school from Christmas vacation. I got dressed. I went outside. The weather was cold. The sky, however, was beautiful. I stood with friends waiting for the school bus. On the bus I summarized for my friends what I had done over the holidays. The bus pulled into the school parking lot. I got out and joined the throngs of students entering the school.

PRACTICE 16

Select twenty sentences from writing you have done recently, from the same piece or from different pieces. Choose ten of the sentences to expand. For each of the ten, add at least one expansion. Vary the lengths, structures, and positions of the expansions.

5
Paragraph Expanding

DEFINING PARAGRAPH EXPANDING

Paragraph expanding is an excellent way to apply the sentence composing techniques studied in earlier sections of the book. The emphasis here is the same as it has been throughout the book: practice in dealing with mature sentence structures. Paragraph expanding approximates more closely the act of writing from scratch: the composing of sentences as integral to the composing of paragraphs.

Like the earlier sections in the book, this section relies on the writing of professionals, but to a lesser extent. After reviewing paragraph unity, paragraph organization, and consistency of style, you will be given paragraphs from which some sentences have been deleted. You are to insert sentences of your own that are compatible with the rest of the sentences.

Paragraph expanding provides more independence from the sentences of professional writers and places greater demands on your skills. In paragraph expanding you are collaborating with the writer into whose paragraph you insert your own sentences. Both of you, working together, create a well-written paragraph.

PARAGRAPH UNITY

Compare the two series of sentences below. Both have the surface appearance of paragraphs: consecutive arrangement of sentences and similarity of subject matter. Only one, however, is a paragraph, with the proper interrelationship among the sentences. The other lacks that interrelationship; and even though its sentences by themselves are well-written and all refer to the same topic in some way, it is a non-paragraph, a jumble of disconnected thoughts.

A.   Lacrosse is an increasingly popular sport in all parts of the country. The word lacrosse comes from two French words: "la" (meaning "the") and "crosse" (meaning a crutch), which a lacrosse stick looks like. Even people who are familiar with lacrosse don't know that it's one of the oldest games played in the United States; it was first played by North American Indians centuries ago. In many schools lacrosse is offered only as a women's sport in the spring, even though it's a physically demanding game—hard on the lungs, the legs, the arms, and even the head when an opponent's stick is used as a weapon. Field sizes differ, as in soccer; but no matter how large a field is, there's no escaping a flailing racket if you don't get rid of the ball quickly enough.

B. The third annual crafts fair at the Baltimore Civic Center was even better attended than the first two, with over twenty-five thousand visitors during its three day run, people from all over, some from as far away as San Francisco. Over two hundred artists displayed their crafts: soft sculptures usable as pillows or wall decorations; jewelry made of multi-colored feathers, artistically arranged in both symmetrical and random patterns; glass art in contemporary designs of simple geometric shapes; and everything from brooms to brocades. Browsers and buyers strolled from booth to booth. The artists were cordial to both groups, from the ignorant who couldn't distinguish between a finely wrought ceramic pot and the old pots they had thrown out as junk during spring cleaning, to the art critics from the local newspapers whose appreciation was based on solid knowledge of craft technique.

The true paragraph is a series of interrelated sentences; the other is just a listing of information about lacrosse. A unified paragraph is not just a container for loosely related ideas, but rather a container whose ideas are interrelated, tied together in a clear and orderly way.

PRACTICE 1

Choose one of the five sentences from the non-paragraph and add two sentences to create a unified three-sentence paragraph.

Sentence from Non-Paragraph

Field sizes differ, as in soccer; but no matter how large a field is, there's no escaping a flailing racket if you don't get rid of the ball quickly enough.

Expanded Version (Two Sentences Added)

To a non-player, lacrosse looks like a cross-country exercise in legal mayhem. The person running with the ball carefully cradled in the twisting racket pouch is pursued across the turf by a band of stick-wielding maniacs. **Field sizes differ, as in soccer; but no matter how large a field is, there's no escaping a flailing racket if you don't get rid of the ball quickly enough.**

Now the sentence from the non-paragraph, joined by two related sentences, contributes to the unity of the paragraph. The three sentences have a "container"—one topic that gives the series of sentences an interrelationship: the potential for "legal mayhem" in lacrosse.

Create a similar context for your choice of one of these sentences:

1. Lacrosse is an increasingly popular sport in all parts of the country.

2. The word lacrosse comes from two French words: "la" (meaning "the") and "crosse" (meaning a crutch), which a lacrosse stick looks like.

3. Even people who are familiar with lacrosse don't know that it's one of the oldest games played in the United States; it was first played by North American Indians centuries ago.

4. In many schools lacrosse is offered only as a women's sport in the spring, even though it's a physically demanding game—hard on the lungs, the legs, the arms, and even the head when an opponent's stick is used as a weapon.

5. Field sizes differ, as in soccer; but no matter how large a field is, there's no escaping a flailing racket if you don't get rid of the ball quickly enough.

The following paragraph series is from Ernest Hemingway's *The Old Man and the Sea,* the story of an old man, Santiago, who struggles courageously with the elements of nature alone at sea but who, in the end, is physically and emotionally exhausted, perhaps to the point of death. The excerpt, a series of five paragraphs, illustrates unity among the paragraphs (inter-paragraph unity), with all five paragraphs supporting the central idea (the exhaustion of Santiago). In turn, all of the sentences within each paragraph (intra-paragraph unity) contribute to the central idea of, first, the respective paragraphs of which they are part and, second, the central idea of the paragraph series. Read the paragraph series several times, noticing how each sentence contributes to the unity of each paragraph and how each paragraph contributes to the unity of the central idea of the paragraph series.

Paragraph One

1. He unstepped the mast and furled the sail and tied it. 2. Then he shouldered the mast and started to climb. 3. It was then he knew the depth of his tiredness. 4. He stopped for a moment and looked back and saw in the reflection from the street light the great tail of the fish standing up well behind the skiff's stern. 5. He saw the white naked line of his backbone and the dark mass of the head with the projecting bill and all the nakedness between.

Paragraph Two

6. He started to climb again and at the top fell and lay for some time with the mast across his shoulder. 7. He tried to get up. 8. But it was too difficult and he sat there with the mast on his shoulder and looked at the road. 9. A cat

passed on the far side going about its business and the old man watched it. 10. Then he just watched the road.

Paragraph Three

11. Finally he put the mast down and stood up. 12. He picked the mast up and put it on his shoulder and started up the road. 13. He had to sit down five times before he reached his shack.

Paragraph Four

14. Inside the shack he leaned the mast against the wall. 15. In the dark he found a water bottle and took a drink. 16. Then he lay down on the bed. 17. He pulled the blanket over his shoulders and then over his back and legs and he slept face down on the newspapers with his arms out straight and the palms of his hands up.

Paragraph Five

18. He was asleep when the boy looked in the door in the morning. 19. It was blowing so hard that the drifting-boats would not be going out and the boy had slept late and then come to the old man's shack as he had come each morning. 20. The boy saw that the old man was breathing and then he saw the old man's hands and he started to cry. 21. He went out very quietly to go to bring some coffee and all the way down the road he was crying.

It is obvious that the five-paragraph series develops the central idea of Santiago's exhaustion. Furthermore, each of the five paragraphs has its own unity, a central idea that ties all the sentences together. Which paragraph develops each central idea?

1. Santiago's first awareness of his exhaustion?
2. Another person's confirmation of his exhaustion?
3. The first demonstration for the reader of his exhaustion?
4. The outcome of his exhaustion?
5. A further demonstration for the reader of his exhaustion?

The sentences in the five paragraphs are remarkably alike: relatively short and uncomplicated in structure. How does this *intentional* sameness reinforce the central idea of the paragraph series (Santiago's exhaustion)?

Unity in paragraphs, as you can see, is of two kinds: intra-paragraph, in which the sentences develop the central idea of a paragraph; and inter-paragraph, in which the paragraphs in a series develop the central idea of the series. The result is a network of unified meaning.

PRACTICE 2

The purpose of this Practice is to add sentences to the given sentence to create a unified paragraph. For each sentence, add content and structure suggested by the given sentence that will blend smoothly with the given sentence. The position to use for the given sentence is indicated: if the given sentence is designated "First sentence," add a second and third; if it is a "Second sentence," add a first and third; if "Third sentence," add a first and second. Compare your result with the original three-sentence series in the References.

Sentence by Professional Writer

The Glasses had a fifth-story apartment, a story higher than the school building, and at this hour the sun was shining over the school roof and through the Glasses' naked living-room windows.

J. D. Salinger, Franny and Zooey

Example (First Sentence)

The Glasses had a fifth-story apartment, a story higher than the school building, and at this hour the sun was shining over the school roof and through the Glasses' naked living-room windows. **One of the Glass children, the youngest, pressed his nose against the window, his eyes staring at the bus stop, where he watched for his uncle to arrive at any minute. Standing there, statue-like, he waited for the bus to appear at the corner of the school building and deposit his uncle safely home.**

Of course, there is no way for you to know the original content in the three sentences of the professional writer; you are given only one sentence from which you have to imagine content that will blend with what *is* given. The purpose is not to duplicate the professional writer's content and sentence structure but to create a smooth blend with what the professional has provided. The result will be a unified paragraph.

Paragraph Written by the Professional Writer

The Glasses had a fifth-story apartment, a story higher than the school building, and at this hour the sun was shining over the school roof and through the Glasses' naked living-room windows. **Sunshine was very unkind to the room. Not only were the furnishings old, intrinsically unlovely, and clotted with memory and sentiment, but the room itself in past years had served as the arena for countless hockey and football (tackle as well as "touch") games, and there was scarcely a leg on any piece of furniture that wasn't badly nicked or marred.**

J. D. Salinger, Franny and Zooey

Salinger's sentences and the student's are different in content and structure, but they are *alike* in that they provide a unity for a three-sentence paragraph and are effective in structure and in content.

1.   The admiral was now faced with a decision no man should have to make. (First sentence)

James A. Michener, The Bridges at Toko-Ri

2.   Montag heard the voices talking, talking, talking, giving, talking, weaving, reweaving their hypnotic web. (Third sentence)

Ray Bradbury, Fahrenheit 451

3.   In my imagination I saw armies of ants and cockroaches calling to one another and scurrying toward my head, to some place under the top of my skull, where they would build new nests. (Second sentence)

Jerzy Kosinski, The Painted Bird

4.   He woke just after two and heard the wind. (First sentence)

Daphne du Maurier, The Birds

5.   A silence, unusual and depressing, settled upon all three, which lasted until the old couple arose to retire for the night. (Third sentence)

W. W. Jacobs, "The Monkey's Paw"

6.   The following day the animal passed away, most likely of internal injuries, on the corner of Mariposa and Fulton streets. (Second sentence)

William Saroyan, My Name Is Aram

7.   All eyes turned to look down the street where a figure had suddenly materialized in the darkness, and the sound of measured footsteps on concrete grew louder and louder as it walked toward them. (Second sentence)

Rod Serling, "The Monsters Are Due on Maple Street"

PARAGRAPH ORGANIZATION

Look again at the paragraph series from *The Old Man and the Sea.* Read the paragraphs in any other order than the original and see that, although they all focus on Santiago's exhaustion, they *have to* appear in the original order. Discuss why.

PRACTICE 3

The following paragraph series are disorganized, purposely scrambled for you to unscramble to produce a pattern of inter-paragraph organization. List the correct order, explain your reasons, and check the References to see the way the professional writer organized the paragraph series. Your order, even though it may differ from the professional writer's, is acceptable if it shows a logical pattern of inter-paragraph organization.

1a.   Big Moe called the Mayor and demanded that something be done to make the streets safe for trucks. "This is very bad for business," said Big Moe. "Another week of this, and I will be out of business."

b.   Except for the truck drivers, of course. Three were quick to see that it would be dangerous to keep the trucks off the streets for more than a few days. Once people became accustomed to having the freedom of the streets again, they would object to the return of the trucks. The Three agreed that it was imperative to get the trucks back on the streets as fast as possible.

c.   All the pushcarts were back on the streets, and the pushcart peddlers did more business on that day than they had for nineteen years. The whole city was jubilant.

From paragraphs by Jean Merrill, The Pushcart War

2a.   In the kitchen the breakfast stove gave a hissing sigh and ejected from its warm interior eight pieces of perfectly browned toast, eight eggs sunnyside up, sixteen slices of bacon, two coffees, and two cool glasses of milk.

b.   "Today is August 4, 2026," said a second voice from the kitchen ceiling, "in the city of Allendale, California." It repeated the date three times for memory's sake. "Today is Mr. Featherstone's birthday. Today is the anniversary of Tilita's marriage. Insurance is payable, as are the water, gas, and light bills."

c.   In the living room the voice-clock sang, *Tick-tock seven o'clock, time to get up, time to get up, seven o'clock!* as if it were afraid that nobody would. The morning house lay empty. The clock ticked on, repeating and repeating its sounds into the emptiness. *Seven-nine, breakfast time, seven-nine!*

From paragraphs by Ray Bradbury, "There Will Come Soft Rains"

3a.   They said it again.

b.   The President's white hair was awry; his eyes had the sleep-hung look of a man in need of more rest. His brain, however, came wide awake.

c.   The President of the United States was awakened after a conference. When they told him, he reached for his dressing gown, started to get up, and then sat on the edge of his bed. "Say that again."

From paragraphs by Philip Wylie, "The Answer"

4a.   The girl had on a white dress. She curved in and she curved out. Her waist went in to a span as narrow and supple as a grapevine; elsewhere she had the fullness of the clusters. Her hair was like Oral's, but her eyes when she had looked up at Emmett were like the best milk-agates he had ever owned. O God, Emmett silently prayed, I thank thee for not letting me stay home and study mules.

b.   The girl looked up at Emmett, then grated away, not saying a word. Emmett prepared to speak, but could not for a minute. He knew what a beautiful girl should look like; he had often thought about it; he knew exactly what it took. So far as he could see, nothing was missing.

c.   She was a calm-looking girl, but seeing Emmett, she dropped the nutmeg, and the sound it made rolling along the bare floor boards brought him back to speech.

d.   And there was a girl in the room. Emmett saw her last of all. She stood
in the darkest corner of the room, leaning against the sink, grating nutmeg on
a pudding of some kind. Emmett could smell the vanilla, sweet and sharp,
above the sweet muskiness of the nutmeg.

From paragraphs by Jessamyn West, "A Time of Learning"

As with *inter-paragraph organization,* just demonstrated, there must also be
logically connected order *within* a paragraph, or *intra-paragraph organization.*
Here is a rearrangement of one of Hemingway's paragraphs with sentences
placed at random, showing no clear organizational pattern.

Scrambled Paragraph (Disorganized)

He had to sit down five times before he reached his shack. He picked the mast
up and put it on his shoulder and started up the road. Finally he put the mast
down and stood up.

Original Paragraph (Organized)

Finally he put the mast down and stood up. He picked the mast up and put it
on his shoulder and started up the road. He had to sit down five times before
he reached his shack.

PRACTICE 4

The following sentence series are disorganized, purposely scrambled for you
to unscramble to produce a well-organized paragraph. List the correct order,
explain your reasons, and check the References to see the way the professional writer organized the paragraph. Your order, even though it may differ
from the professional writer's, is acceptable if it shows a logical pattern of
intra-paragraph organization.

1a.   The other, submerged in his overcoat, listened with interest.

 b.   The two men started up the street, arm in arm.

 c.   The man from the West, his egotism enlarged by success, was beginning
to outline the history of his career.

From a paragraph by O. Henry, "After Twenty Years"

2a.   One of the aggrieved privates came forward with his shovel.

 b.   Then the soldier emptied his shovel on—on the feet.

 c.   He lifted his first shovel-load of earth, and for a moment of inexplicable
hesitation it was held poised above this corpse, which from its chalk-blue face
looked keenly out from the grave.

From a paragraph by Stephan Crane, "The Upturned Face"

3a.   In his left hand he held a bottle of brandy.

 b.   The waiter came back into the room carrying a tray with a big coffee
glass and a liqueur glass on it.

c. He swung these down to the table and a boy who had followed him poured coffee and milk into the glass from two shiny, spouted pots with long handles.

From a paragraph by Ernest Hemingway, "The Undefeated"

4a. Once, in the barn, his father had come upon a picture of Emmett's painting.

b. Except for the front of a house, an expanse of white siding dazzling in sunlight, there was almost nothing in the picture at all: shallow wooden steps ascended to a partially open door; beyond the door on the dark floor boards and deep in shadow lay something crumpled, a piece of goods, a ribbon perhaps, and beyond that a naked, retreating heel.

c. He stared at it for a long time.

d. It was a big, empty picture with great reaches of unoccupied cardboard.

From a paragraph by Jessamyn West, "A Time of Learning"

5a. He lunged for it; a short, hoarse cry came from his lips as he realized he had reached too far and had lost his balance.

b. He strained his eyes in the direction from which the reports had come.

c. Rainsford sprang up and moved quickly to the rail, mystified.

d. The cry was pinched off short as the blood-warm waters of the Caribbean Sea closed over his head.

e. He leaped upon the rail and balanced himself there, to get greater elevation; his pipe, striking a rope, was knocked from his mouth.

From a paragraph by Richard Connell, "The Most Dangerous Game"

6a. The Mandarin fell so ill that he had his bed drawn up by the silken screen and there he lay, miserably giving his architectural orders.

b. Sickness spread in the city like a pack of evil dogs.

c. The voice behind the screen was weak now, too, and faint, like the wind in the eaves.

d. Funerals began to appear in the streets, though it was the middle of summer, a time when all should be tending and harvesting.

e. The population, working now steadily for endless months upon the changing of the walls, resembled Death himself, clattering his white bones like musical instruments in the wind.

f. Shops closed.

From a paragraph by Ray Bradbury, "The Golden Kite, the Silver Wind"

7a. His next errand was at Tiffany's, where he selected silver-mounted brushes and a scarf pin.

b. After he reached the Twenty-third Street station, he consulted a cabman, and had himself driven to a men's furnishing establishment which was just opening for the day.

c. He spent upward of two hours there, buying with endless reconsidering and great care.

d.   When he arrived at the Jersey City station, he hurried through his breakfast, manifestly ill at ease and keeping a sharp eye about him.

e.   His new street suit he put on in the fitting room; the frock coat and dress clothes he had bundled into the cab with his new shirts.

f.   Lastly, he stopped at a trunk shop on Broadway, and had his purchases packed into various traveling bags.

g.   Then he drove to a hatter's and a shoe house.

h.   He would not wait to have his silver marked, he said.

From a paragraph by Willa Cather, "Paul's Case"

CONSISTENCY OF STYLE

So far we have seen that well-written paragraphs are unified and organized both within a paragraph and between paragraphs in a series. Another aspect of well-written paragraphs is consistency of style.

Style is similar to personality—those qualities in people that give them uniqueness: ways of walking, ways of talking, disposition, philosophy of life, abilities, talents, interests, and so forth. Style in writing is the "personality" of writing. The mood of the writing is like the mood of a person—perhaps somber, or whimsical, or flippant, or deadly serious. Just as people have individual manners of speaking, writers have individual ways of writing—short and to the point or highly detailed, plain speech or ornate expression, use of common or uncommon words, quick disclosure of main ideas or gradual unfolding of them.

PRACTICE 5

Following are five paragraphs that are representative of consistency of style in the works from which they are taken. Each author has a style that is readily identifiable within the paragraph excerpt and distinguishable from the styles of the four other authors.

Read each paragraph several times, paying special attention to any patterns that occur: ways of beginning sentences, sentence lengths, structures used within sentences, punctuation, and word choice. One sentence has been deleted from each paragraph, a sentence that is consistent with the style already established in the paragraph. Your job is to select from a list of three sentences the one sentence that belongs in the paragraph in the place where the deletion occurs.

A.   1. But the music of the pearl was shrilling with triumph in Kino. 2. Juana looked up, and her eyes were wide at Kino's courage and at his imagination. 3. And electric strength had come to him now the horizons were kicked out. 4. In the pearl he saw Coyotito sitting at a little desk in a school, just as Kino had once seen it through an open door. 5. *(Deletion)* 6. Moreover, Coyotito was writing on a big piece of paper. 7. Kino looked at his neighbors fiercely. 8. "My son will go to school," he said, and the neighbors were hushed. 9. Juana caught her breath sharply. 10. Her eyes were bright as she watched him, and she looked quickly down at Coyotito in her arms to see whether this might be possible.

John Steinbeck, *The Pearl*

Which sentence is most consistent with the style of the rest of the sentences in the paragraph? Why?

a. Coyotito, wearing a white collar and broad silken tie, was dressed in a jacket.

b. And Coyotito was dressed in a jacket, and he had on a white collar and a broad silken tie.

c. Dressed in a jacket which had once been Kino's, Coyotito also wore a starched, newly-cleaned white collar and a broad and brightly colored silken tie.

B. 1. It began one evening after supper. 2. *(Deletion)* 3. It had been a placid week. 4. I had minded Aunty; Jem had outgrown the treehouse, but helped Dill and me construct a new rope ladder for it; Dill had hit upon a foolproof plan to make Boo Radley come out at no cost to ourselves (place a trail of lemon drops from the back door to the front yard and he'd follow it, like an ant). 5. There was a knock on the front door; Jem answered it and said it was Mr. Heck Tate.

Harper Lee, *To Kill a Mockingbird*

Which sentence is most consistent with the style of the rest of the sentences in the paragraph? Why?

a. Dill came over to the house, and Aunt Alexandra was in her chair in the corner, and Atticus was in his, and Jem and I were on the floor reading.

b. Dill, Aunt Alexandra, Atticus, Jem, and I were all home.

c. Dill was over; Aunt Alexandra was in her chair in the corner; Atticus was in his; Jem and I were on the floor reading.

C. 1. It made a single last leap into the air coming down at Montag from a good three feet over his head, its spidered legs reaching, the procaine needle snapping out its single angry tooth. 2. Montag caught it with a bloom of fire, a single wondrous blossom that curled in petals of yellow and blue and orange about the metal dog, clad it in a new covering as it slammed into Montag and threw him ten feet back against the bole of a tree, taking the flame-gun with him. 3. *(Deletion)* 4. Montag lay watching the dead-alive thing fiddle the air and die. 5. Even now it seemed to want to get back at him and finish the injection which was now working through the flesh of his leg.

Ray Bradbury, Fahrenheit 451

Which sentence is most consistent with the style of the rest of the sentences in the paragraph? Why?

a.   It landed, stabbing its deadly needle into his leg.

b.   Before the fire killed the monstrous metal dog, bursting its metal bones at the joints, he felt it scrabble and seize his leg and stab the needle in for a moment.

c.   He felt it scrabble and seize his leg and stab the needle in for a moment before the fire snapped the hound up in the air, burst its metal bones at the joints, and blew out its interior in a single flushing of red color like a skyrocket fastened to the street.

D.   1. Indeed, as I learned, there were on the planet where the little prince lived—as on all planets—good plants and bad plants. 2. *(Deletion)* 3. But seeds are invisible. 4. They sleep deep in the heart of the earth's darkness, until some one among them is seized with the desire to awaken. 5. Then this little seed will stretch itself and begin—timidly at first—to push a charming little sprig inoffensively upward toward the sun. 6. If it is only a sprout of radish or the sprig of a rose-bush, one would let it grow wherever it might wish. 7. But when it is a bad plant, one must destroy it as soon as possible, the very first instant one recognizes it.

Antoine de Saint Exupéry, The Little Prince

Which sentence is most consistent with the style of the rest of the sentences in the paragraph? Why?

a.   In consequence, there were good seeds from good plants, and bad seeds from bad plants.

b.   So there were good seeds, and some of them were bad seeds.

c.   There were good and bad seeds from good and bad plants.

E.   1. But to accept this rage and misery as a source of comfort is to enter one of the vicious circles of hell. 2. *(Deletion)* 3. Because one cannot forgive oneself, one cannot forgive others, or, even, really, *see* others—one is always striking out at the wrong person, for only some other, poor, doomed innocent, obviously, is likely to be in striking range. 4. One's self-esteem begins to shrivel; one's hope for the future begins to crack. 5. In reacting against what the world calls you, you endlessly validate its judgment.

James Baldwin, "Every Good-bye Ain't Gone"

Which sentence is most consistent with the style of the rest of the sentences in the paragraph? Why?

a.   You can't forgive the world for this horror, and you can't forgive yourself.

b.   One does not forgive the world nor oneself for this horror.

c.   One does not, after all, forgive the world for this horror, nor can one forgive oneself.

PRACTICE 6

The following five passages were taken from the same works as were those in the last Practice. Now that you have identified sentences consistent with the author's style, you should be able to match the five authors with the new passages below. Explain your selections.

Sources

1.   James Baldwin, "Every Good-bye Ain't Gone"

2.   Ray Bradbury, *Fahrenheit 451*

3.   Antoine de Saint Exupéry, *The Little Prince*

4.   Harper Lee, *To Kill a Mockingbird*

5.   John Steinbeck, *The Pearl*

Passages

A.   1. Now my sorrow is comforted a little. 2. That is to say—not entirely. 3. But I know that he did go back to his planet, because I did not find his body at daybreak. 4. It was not such a heavy body . . . . 5. And at night I love to listen to the stars. 6. It is like five hundred million little bells . . . .

B.   1. The power of the social definition is that it becomes, fatally, one's own—but it took time, and much deep water, to make me see this. 2. Rage and misery can be a source of comfort, simply because one has lived with rage and misery for so long.

C.   1. He was a curiosity. 2. He wore blue linen shorts that buttoned to his shirt; his hair was snow white and stuck to his head like duckfluff; he was a year my senior but I towered over him. 3. As he told us the old tale his blue eyes would lighten and darken; his laugh was sudden and happy; he habitually pulled at a cowlick in the center of his forehead.

D.   1. But he was suspicious, and he could not take his eyes from the doctor's open bag, and from the bottle of white powder there. 2. Gradually the spasms subsided and the baby relaxed under the doctor's hands. 3. And then the baby sighed deeply and went to sleep, for he was very tired with vomiting.

E.   1. And the men with the cigarettes in their straight-lined mouths, the men with the eyes of puff adders, took up their load of machine and tube, their case of liquid melancholy and the slow dark sludge of nameless stuff, and strolled out the door.

REVIEW

PRACTICE 7

This Practice reviews the three characteristics of well-written paragraphs: (1) unity, (2) organization, and (3) consistency of style.

The following scrambled list of sentences is taken from three different paragraphs by three different writers, each of whom has a unique writing style. Your task is to reconstruct the three original paragraphs: to decide which sentences have a common style and central topic, and to arrange those sentences in a logical sequence to organize the paragraph.

The sources of the paragraphs are Ray Bradbury, *The Martian Chronicles;* Harper Lee, *To Kill a Mockingbird;* and Edgar Allan Poe, "The Cask of Amontillado." When you finish, compare your three paragraphs with the original three in the References.

1.   His hair was dead and thin, almost feathery on top of his head.

2.   At the summit of the house was a cupola with diamond leaded-glass windows and a dunce-cap roof.

3.   Three sides of this interior crypt were still ornamented in this manner.

4.   Within the wall thus exposed by the displacing of the bones, we perceived a still interior recess, in depth about four feet, in width three, in height six or seven.

5.   The rocket landed on a lawn of green grass.

6.   His face was as white as his hands, but for a shadow on his jutting chin.

7.   Through the front window you could see a piece of music titled "Beautiful Ohio" sitting on the music rest.

8.   It seemed to have been constructed for no especial use within itself, but formed merely the interval between two of the colossal supports of the roof of the catacombs, and was backed by one of their circumscribing walls of solid granite.

9.   At the most remote end of the crypt there appeared another less spacious.

10.   Upon the porch were hairy geraniums and an old swing which was hooked into the porch ceiling which now swung back and forth, back and forth, in a little breeze.

11.   Outside, upon this lawn, stood an iron deer.

12. His cheeks were thin to hollowness; his mouth was wide; there were shallow, almost delicate indentations at his temples, and his gray eyes were so colorless I thought he was blind.

13. I looked from his hands to his sand-stained khaki pants; my eyes traveled up his thin frame to his torn denim shirt.

14. Further up on the green stood a tall brown Victorian house, quiet in the sunlight, all covered with scrolls and rococo, its windows made of blue and pink and yellow and green colored glass.

15. Its walls had been lined with human remains piled to the vault overhead, in the fashion of the great catacombs of Paris.

16. From the fourth the bones had been thrown down, and lay promiscuously upon the earth, forming at one point a mound of some size.

PRACTICING PARAGRAPH EXPANDING

In paragraph expanding you can learn much that will reinforce the sentence composing techniques you have learned in previous sections of the book; in addition, you can learn much about paragraph composing: how to unify the paragraph by including only sentences that relate to the central idea of the paragraph, how to organize the paragraph by logically sequencing the sentence series that makes up the paragraph, and how to achieve consistency of style.

Paragraph with Deletion

And at night was the most enjoyable time, because when he passed the storekeepers sitting outside their stores, he could tell they regarded him highly. *(Place your sentence here.)*

From a paragraph by Bernard Malamud, "A Summer's Reading"

Sample Student Paragraph Expansions

1. And at night was the most enjoyable time, because when he passed the storekeepers sitting outside their stores, he could tell they regarded him highly. **He strolled the sidewalk, humming, smiling, sometimes stopping to chat.**

2. And at night was the most enjoyable time, because when he passed the storekeepers sitting outside their stores, he could tell they regarded him highly. **One especially, the shoe salesman Mr. Pauley, always demanded a conversation, for Mr. Pauley claimed that every time he talked with that boy he learned some of the things the boy had learned at college, which he himself had always wanted to attend, but never had.**

3. And at night was the most enjoyable time, because when he passed the storekeepers sitting outside their stores, he could tell they regarded him highly. **Inside, though, he felt a gnawing guilt, the result of his sense of hypocrisy about cheating Mrs.** Gramsky **by over-charging her for her laundry, the woman who, along with her husband and kids, was always on the stoop evenings and always spoke to him, certainly admired him, and used him as an example for her own kids.**

Original Paragraph by Professional Writer

And at night was the most enjoyable time, because when he passed the storekeepers sitting outside their stores, he could tell they regarded him highly. **He walked erect, and though he did not say much to them, or they to him, he could feel approval on all sides.**

Notice that from one student's sentence to the next, there is a great variety in the sentences the students added to the sentence by the professional writer: different contents, sentence lengths, and sentence structures. Furthermore, all three differ from Malamud's original sentence. Nevertheless, all three student sentences are acceptable; all three in content and in style blend smoothly with the professional writer's sentence. The only *essential* requirement for the sentences you add is that they be compatible with the content and style of the sentences by the professional writer.

PRACTICE 8

Expand the paragraphs below by composing sentences that match the description of the original sentences that have been deleted. Part of the description includes the suggested length for your sentence, based on the actual length of the deleted sentence:

Short: 1–15 words
Medium: 16–30 words
Long: 31–50 words

The second part of the description is the general topic. In addition to following the suggested length and topic, compose your sentences in a style that is consistent with the professional writer's.

Paragraph with Deletions (Description of *Tyrannosaurus rex*)

1. It came on great oiled, resilient, striding legs.
2. It towered thirty feet above half of the trees, a great evil god, folding its delicate watchmaker's claws close to its oily reptilian chest.
3. *Length: Medium. Topic: Its Lower Legs.*
4. Each thigh was a ton of meat, ivory, and steel mesh.
5. *Length: Medium. Topic: Its Arms, Its Neck.*

6. *Length: Short. Topic: Its Head.*

7. *Length: Short. Topic: Its Mouth.*

8. *Length: Short. Topic: Its Eyes.*

9. It closed its mouth in a death grin.

10. It ran, its pelvic bones crushing aside trees and bushes, its taloned feet clawing damp earth, leaving prints six inches deep wherever it settled its weight.

11. It ran with a gliding ballet step, far too poised and balanced for its ten tons.

12. It moved into a sunlit arena warily, its beautifully reptile hands feeling the air.

From a paragraph by Ray Bradbury, "A Sound of Thunder"

The sentences provided by the professional writer should be considered a magnet, drawing from your sentence composing skill a style that is comparable to that of the professional. Since you are, in effect, a partner of that writer, you will want to write the best sentences you can. If your sentences are noticeably inferior, the overall quality of the paragraph will be considerably reduced, like putting cheap plastic flowers in a fine gold vase.

The purpose of paragraph expanding, and the reason this section is placed last in the book, is to give you a chance to use all of the sentence composing techniques and skills you have learned in earlier sections to produce sentences that are indistinguishable from those of professional writers.

Sample Student Paragraph Expansion

1. It came on great oiled, resilient, striding legs. 2. It towered thirty feet above half of the trees, a great evil god, folding its delicate watchmaker's claws close to its oily reptilian chest. 3. **Its lower legs, hard concrete muscles pounding the dense foliage, moved powerfully throughout the jungle.** 4. Each thigh was a ton of meat, ivory, and steel mesh. 5. **The strange tiny arms, scaled and groping wildly at the treetops, snapped off huge branches, as if they were twigs, its spring-like neck bobbing gently, grotesquely.** 6. **Its head, a bag of stones enveloped in wrinkles, dangled.** 7. **Its mouth, in a frozen frown, suggested rigor mortis.** 8. **Two balls of putrid jelly, the eyes blinked.** 9. It closed its mouth in a death grin. 10. It ran, its pelvic bones crushing aside trees and bushes, its taloned feet clawing damp earth, leaving prints six inches deep wherever it settled its weight. 11. It ran with a gliding ballet step, far too poised and balanced for its ten tons. 12. It moved into a sunlit arena warily, its beautifully reptile hands feeling the air.

The student succeeds in composing sentences that blend well with the professional writer's, both in content and in style.

Note: The guidelines for sentence lengths are only suggestions based on the length of the original sentence. In the fifth sentence, above, the student exceeded the suggested length (short) but composed an excellent sentence.

Original Paragraph

1. It came on great oiled, resilient, striding legs. 2. It towered thirty feet above half of the trees, a great evil god, folding its delicate watchmaker's claws close to its oily reptilian chest. 3. **Each lower leg was a piston, a thousand pounds of white bone, sunk in thick ropes of muscle, sheathed over in a gleam of pebbled skin like the mail of a terrible warrior.** 4. Each thigh was a ton of meat, ivory, and steel mesh. 5. **And from the great breathing cage of the upper body those two delicate arms dangled out front, arms with hands which might pick up and examine men like toys, while the snake neck coiled.** 6. **And the head itself, a ton of sculptured stone, lifted easily upon the sky.** 7. **Its mouth gaped, exposing a fence of teeth like daggers.** 8. **Its eyes rolled, ostrich eggs, empty of all expression save hunger.** 9. It closed its mouth in a death grin. 10. It ran, its pelvic bones crushing aside trees and bushes, its taloned feet clawing damp earth, leaving prints six inches deep wherever it settled its weight. 11. It ran with a gliding ballet step, far too poised and balanced for its ten tons. 12. It moved into a sunlit arena warily, its beautifully reptile hands feeling the air.

Add sentences below that will contribute to the paragraph's unity, organization, and stylistic consistency.

A. From *The Red Pony* by John Steinbeck, a paragraph describing the morning exercise of a pony.

1. Every morning, after Jody had curried and brushed the pony, he let down the barrier of the stall, and Gabilan thrust past him and raced down the barn and into the corral.

2. *Length: Short. Topic: The Pony in Motion.*

3. *Length: Medium. Topic: The Pony Not in Motion.*

4. *Length: Medium. Topic: The Pony Drinking from the Trough.*

5. Jody was proud then, for he knew that was the way to judge a horse.

6. Poor horses only touched their lips to the water, but a fine spirited beast put his whole nose and mouth under, and only left room to breathe.

B. From *Gone With the Wind* by Margaret Mitchell, a paragraph describing the physical appearance of the heroine of the story:

1. Scarlett O'Hara was not beautiful, but men seldom realized it when caught by her charm as the Tarleton twins were.

2. In her face were too sharply blended the delicate features of her mother, a Coast aristocrat of French descent, and the heavy ones of her florid Irish father.

3. But it was an arresting face, pointed of chin, square of jaw.

4. *Length: Medium. Topic: Her Eyes.*

5. *Length: Long. Topic: Her Eyebrows, Her Beautiful Skin.*

C. From *A Modern Instance* by William Dean Howells, a paragraph describing winter:

1. But winter was full half the year.

2. *Length: Long. Topic: Snow Storms from November to May.*

3. When it did not snow, the weather was keenly clear, and commonly very still.

4. *Length: Long. Topic: Typical Beautiful Sunny Winter Day.*

5. On such days the farmers and lumbermen came in to the village stores, and made a stiff and feeble stir about their doorways, and the school children gave the street a little life and color, as they went to and from the Academy in their red and blue woolens.

D. From "The Eighty-Yard Run" by Irwin Shaw, a paragraph describing a football player's run down the field for a touchdown:

1. The pass was high and wide and he jumped for it, feeling it slap flatly against his hands, as he shook his hips to throw off the half-back who was diving at him.

2. The center floated by, his hands desperately brushing Darling's knee as Darling picked his feet up high and delicately ran over a blocker and an opposing linesman in a jumble on the ground near the scrimmage line.

3. *Length: Long. Topic: Various Attempts to Tackle Him.*

4. He smiled a little to himself as he ran, holding the ball lightly in front of him with his two hands, his knees pumping high, his hips twisting in the almost girlish run of a back in a broken field.

5. *Length: Long. Topic: Halfback's Attempt to Tackle Him.*

6. There was only the safety man now, coming warily at him, his arms crooked, hands spread.

7. *Length: Medium. Topic: Preparing for His Evasion of Safety Man.*

8. He was sure he was going to get past the safety man.

9. *Length: Long. Topic: Confrontation with Safety Man.*

10. He pivoted away, keeping the arm locked, dropping the safety man as he ran easily toward the goal line, with the drumming of cleats diminishing behind him.

In the next series of paragraph-expanding Practices, fewer of the sentences from a paragraph by the professional writer are provided, creating more of a challenge. Although some general guidelines for unity, organization, and style are provided, in these Practices you will have to be more self-reliant than in previous paragraph-expanding Practices. When you compare your finished paragraph with that of the professional writer, expect differences: there is no way that such differences can be avoided, nor should they be. You are not imitating the structure or content of the professional writer's sentences. What you *are* imitating is something far more important, the writer's *process* of creation—the ability, not the specific achievement.

PRACTICE 9

Both exercises in this expanding Practice are elaborate descriptions of types of food, one describing the array of foods in an appealing indoor delicatessen, the other in a huge outdoor food market.

Before expanding the paragraphs, look at a similar paragraph on food that has the same qualities as the ones you will expand. This paragraph is a listing of the foods displayed in preparation for a family feast.

1. A fat brown goose lay at one end of the table and at the other end, on a bed of creased paper strewn with sprigs of parsley, lay a great ham, stripped of its outer skin and peppered over with crust crumbs, a neat paper frill round its shin and beside this was a round of spiced beef. 2. Between these rival ends ran parallel lines of side-dishes: two little minsters of jelly, red and yellow, a shallow dish full of blocks of blanc-mange and red jam, a large green leaf-shaped dish with a stalk-shaped handle, on which lay bunches of purple raisins and peeled almonds, a companion dish on which lay a solid rectangle of Smyrna figs, a dish of custard topped with grated nutmeg, a small bowl full of chocolates and sweets wrapped in gold and silver papers and a glass vase in which stood some tall celery stalks. 3. In the centre of the table there stood, as sentries to a fruit-stand which upheld a pyramid of oranges and American apples, two squat old-fashioned decanters of cut glass, one containing port and the other dark sherry. 4. On the closed square piano a pudding in a huge yellow dish lay in waiting, and behind it were three squads of bottles of stout and ale and minerals, drawn up according to the colours of their uniforms, the first two black, with brown and red labels, the third and smallest squad white, with transverse green sashes.

James Joyce, "The Dead"

Paragraph Unity

It is obvious that the paragraph is unified through the development of just one topic: foods displayed in preparation for a feast. The unity is skillfully achieved in two ways: the inclusion of many kinds of foods and the vividness of the descriptions of the individual foods.

1. Count the total number of individual foods described in the paragraph. How many are there? How many are in each individual sentence?

2. List each food with its full description. Underline the food once, the description twice.

Food One: <u>A fat brown goose</u>
Food Two: on a bed of creased paper strewn with sprigs of parsley, lay a great ham

In the paragraphs in this Practice for you to expand, achieve unity through the same two techniques: inclusion of many kinds of foods and vividness of the descriptions of individual foods.

Paragraph Organization

Despite the abundant description, there are only three categories of foods described: meats, side-dishes, beverages.

3. The categories are described in that order. Why? What would have been lost if they were described in one of these rearrangements?

a. side-dishes, beverages, meats

b. beverages, side-dishes, meats

4. Within each of these three categories, specific examples are described. What are they? Are the specific examples described in one sentence or are some in one sentence and the rest in other sentences? What do you conclude concerning Joyce's sentence organization?

5. The overall principle of organization is spatial, that is, telling which places were occupied by which foods. Joyce uses transitional expressions to guide the reader from place to place. List all examples of transitional devices that do so. For example:

Transition One: **at one end of the table**

Transition Two: **and at the other end**

The organization of the paragraph is achieved through a logical arrangement of the categories to be described, grouping of related specific examples within the same sentence, and transitional devices to link together the parts of the spatial organization. In the paragraphs in this Practice for you to expand, achieve organization through the same three techniques: arrangement of categories, grouping of examples, and use of transitional devices.

Consistency of Style

The style of this paragraph reinforces its unity and organization. The feast was elaborate; so too is the style of the writer in describing it.

6.   Only one of the sentences begins with the subject word of the clause with no introductory structures preceding it: "A fat brown goose lay . . . ." This sentence pattern is the most usual for English sentences. Why do you think Joyce avoids this pattern in all of the remaining sentences of the paragraph?

7.   How does consistency in sentence length contribute to the central unifying idea of the description—the elaborateness of the feast?

8.   Although there is consistency in sentence length, there is variety in sentence structure. Give examples of the variety in sentence structure and explain how the variety contributes to the central unifying idea of the description—the elaborateness of the feast.

9.   The writer is consistent in appealing to the reader's eye. List words that describe size or shape (*fat* goose, *great* ham); condition (*creased* paper, *neat* paper frill); color (*brown* goose, *red* jam).

The consistency of style within the paragraph creates a single impression: that the elaborate feast *was appealing.* In the paragraphs in this Practice for you to expand, achieve consistency of style through the same techniques: use of long descriptive sentences varied in structure and use of words that appeal to the reader's eye.

     The first paragraph-expanding Practice below is a description of a delicatessen; the second, a description of an outdoor market. Both are similar to the paragraph describing the elaborate feast analyzed above. In the two descriptions below, add sentences that will similarly achieve unity, organization, and stylistic consistency within the paragraphs.

Description of a Delicatessen

From *The Confessions of Felix Krull* by Thomas Mann:

. . . Down in the town on a corner of what was, comparatively speaking, our busiest street, there was a neat and attractively stocked delicatessen store, a branch, if I am not mistaken, of a Wiesbaden firm. It was patronized by the best society. My way to school led me past this shop daily and I had stopped in many times, coin in hand, to buy cheap candies, fruit drops or barley sugar. But on going in one day I found it empty not only of customers but of attendants as well. There was a little bell on a spring over the door, and this had rung as I entered; but either the inner room was empty or its occupants had not heard the bell—I was and remained alone. The glass door at the rear was covered by some pleated material. At first the emptiness surprised and startled me; it even gave me an uncanny feeling; but presently I began to look about me, for never before had I been able to contemplate undisturbed the delights of such a spot. It was a narrow room, with a rather high ceiling, and crowded from floor to ceiling with goodies. *(Your sentences are inserted here.)*

Directions

Add a total of six sentences to the above paragraph. Some sentences should describe the array of foods on the floor-to-ceiling shelves in the store. Some sentences should describe in great detail the contents of the refrigerated glass showcases. Some sentences should describe the contents on the tops of tables. The description should be elaborate; the sentences, long; the word choice, appealing to the reader's eye. When you finish, compare your paragraph expansion to the original paragraph in the References.

Consecutive Paragraphs Describing Market Sheds

From *Bare Feet in the Palace* by Agnes Newton Keith:

A.   Today, under the long skylit roofs of the market sheds, the long trestle tables are spread with miles of food. *(Your sentences are inserted here.)*

Directions

Add a total of three sentences to the above paragraph. One sentence should describe meats; one, vegetables; one, fruits. The description should be elaborate; the sentences, long; the word choice, appealing to the reader's eye. When you finish, compare your paragraph expansion to the original paragraph in the References.

B.   But more important than anything else, for it is the manna of the Philippines, there are fish in the fishmarket. *(Your sentences are inserted here.)*

Directions

Add a total of five sentences to the above paragraph. Somewhere within the five sentences include descriptions of the following: the variety of Crustacea (shellfish); an overview of the sights and smells of the fishmarket; a vivid visual description of octopuses for sale; methods used to preserve fish (dried, fresh, cured, and so forth); and the range of sizes and the variations in shapes of the fish. The description should be elaborate; the sentences, long; the word choice, appealing to the reader's eye. When you finish, compare your paragraph expansion to the original paragraph in the References.

REVIEWING AND APPLYING PARAGRAPH EXPANDING

Like all of the sentence composing techniques studied in earlier parts of the book, paragraph expanding relies on some help from professional writers; but the reliance is much less, intentionally so, for it is a technique to "wean" you away from the models of professional writers and to establish your own sentence composing style.

In the next series of Practices you will have an opportunity to see to what extent you have mastered the goal of the book: competence in sentence composing skill unaided by professional writers. It is an opportunity to apply the skills from previous sections of the book in a more independent way, but, at the same time, it is more difficult since you are responsible for making more choices. However, this range of choice approximates the reality of writing, a process in which selection among options is ongoing.

PRACTICE 10

In this Practice you are responsible for providing the entire paragraph except for one sentence. All of the choices are yours: content, organization, and style. Sentence lengths, structures, and patterns are also your choice. The only requirement is that you develop your paragraph in a way that is consistent with the essential content and style suggested by the one sentence provided by the professional writer.

The Practice is divided into three sections. The first section provides starting sentences for you to develop with subsequent sentences. The second section provides middle sentences. These are sentences that, in the original paragraphs, were neither the first sentence nor the last but were somewhere between the two. The third section provides ending sentences.

In addition to choosing the content, organization, style, sentence length, structure, and pattern, the length of the paragraph is also your choice. When you finish, compare the choices you have made with the choices made by the professional writers. The original paragraphs are in the References.

Starting Sentences

To expand each paragraph, add sentences that will follow and blend smoothly with the sentence provided, which, in the original, was the first sentence in the paragraph. Do five.

1.　At nearly midnight, the night before the bomb was dropped, an announcer on the city's radio station said that about two hundred B-29s were approaching southern Honshu and advised the population of Hiroshima to evacuate to their designated "safe areas."

From a paragraph by John Hersey, *Hiroshima*

2.　Down on the beach a match flared, and in its momentary light Kino saw that two of the men were sleeping, curled up like dogs, while the third watched, and he saw the glint of the rifle in the match light.

From a paragraph by John Steinbeck, *The Pearl*

3.　The Radley Place had ceased to terrify me, but it was no less gloomy, no less chilly under its great oaks, and no less uninviting.

From a paragraph by Harper Lee, *To Kill A Mockingbird*

4. The concussion knocked the air across and down the river, turned the men over like dominos in a line, blew the water in lifting sprays, and blew the dust and made the trees above them mourn with a great wind passing away south.

From a paragraph by Ray Bradbury, *Fahrenheit 451*

5. While I was waiting around for Phoebe in the museum, right inside the doors and all, these two little kids came up to me and asked me if I knew where the mummies were.

From a paragraph by J. D. Salinger, *The Catcher in the Rye*

6. Then Jody stood and watched the pony, and he saw things he had never noticed about any other horse, the sleek, sliding flank muscles and the cords of the buttocks, which flexed like a closing fist, and the shine the sun put on the red coat.

From a paragraph by John Steinbeck, *The Red Pony*

7. She made breakfast and, when Guy had gone, did the sinkful of dishes and put the kitchen to rights.

From a paragraph by Ira Levin, *Rosemary's Baby*

8. The motorcycle on the sidewalk speeded up and skidded obliquely into a plate-glass window, the front wheel bucking and climbing the brick base beneath the window.

From a paragraph by Frank Rooney, "Cyclists' Raid"

Middle Sentences

To expand each paragraph, add sentences that will precede and sentences that will follow the sentence provided, which, in the original, was somewhere between the first and last sentences of the paragraph. Do five.

9. He ran furiously to and fro, dodging when there was no need to dodge, and in his anxiety to see on every side of him at once, stumbling.

From a paragraph by H. G. Wells, "The Country of the Blind"

10. His waiting room was big and musty and smelled of crayon wax almost as strongly as it smelled of the rubbing alcohol he used to clean the place where he was going to give us a shot.

From a paragraph by Ann Head, *Mr. and Mrs. BoJo Jones*

11. According to Carmen, he wasn't really handsome, but he was nice-looking and a lot of fun.

From a paragraph by Hila Colman, "First Date"

12. The teacher always pronounced his name with profound gusto as she pointed him out as the ideal student.

From a paragraph by John Henrik Clarke, "The Boy Who Painted Christ Black"

13. I had hoped that the white moderate would understand that the present tension in the South is a necessary phase of the transition from an obnoxious negative peace, in which the Negro passively accepted his unjust plight, to a substantive and positive peace, in which all men will respect the dignity and worth of human personality.

From a paragraph by Martin Luther King, Jr., "Letter from Birmingham Jail"

14.   Holding the line with his left shoulder again, and bracing on his left hand and arm, he took the tuna off the gaff hook and put the gaff back in place.

From a paragraph by Ernest Hemingway, The Old Man and the Sea

15.   He motioned Leiber to a chair in his office, gave him a cigar, lit one for himself, sat on the edge of his desk, puffing solemnly for a long moment.

From a paragraph by Ray Bradbury, "The Small Assassin"

16.   The heavy slug struck him in the shoulder and flattened and tore out a piece of his shoulderblade.

From a paragraph by John Steinbeck, East of Eden

Ending Sentences

To expand each paragraph, add sentences that will precede and blend smoothly with the sentence provided, which, in the original, was the last sentence in that paragraph. Do five.

17.   The woman whirled round and fell with a shriek into the gutter.

From a paragraph by Liam O'Flaherty, "The Sniper"

18.   The time was barely ten o'clock at night, but chilly gusts of wind with a taste of rain in them had well nigh depeopled the streets.

From a paragraph by O. Henry, "After Twenty Years"

19.   He was wearing Boy Scout pants and a brown woolen pullover, and on the back of his head was a skullcap made from the crown of a man's felt hat, the edge turned up and cut into sharp points that were ornamented with brass paper clips.

From a paragraph by Murray Heyert, "The New Kid"

20.   The bull watched him, not fixed now, hunting him, but waiting to get close enough so he could be sure of getting him, getting the horns into him.

From a paragraph by Ernest Hemingway, "The Undefeated"

21.   And he smiled pityingly at himself that one of her name should make his pulses stir—for she was an O'Grady.

From a paragraph by Maurice Walsh, "The Quiet Man"

22.   He could hear the soft, slow movements of the animals in their stalls and once in awhile, as the air freshened, a slight fluttering of leaves.

From a paragraph by Jessamyn West, "A Time of Learning"

23.   In his hand the man held a long-barreled revolver, and he was pointing it straight at Rainsford's heart.

From a paragraph by Richard Connell, "The Most Dangerous Game"

24.   He screamed.

From a paragraph by Henry Roth, Call It Sleep

References

INTRODUCTION

1. a
2. b
3. a
4. b
5. b
6. a
7. a

SENTENCE SCRAMBLING

PRACTICE 1 (page 7)

1. b
2. b
3. b
4. a
5. b
6. a
7. b

PRACTICE 3 (pages 9-10)

List One

When the ashtray, which was solid and feathered with grease, sang for him the dance of the petunia and became encouraged to jump up to an ocean and hope for mud, the crab blanked its pencil and covered the floor with its type-writers.

List Two

Although the hamburger, which was crystal and demented in town, ran down to him the story of the onion and seemed reluctant to fly away in a dictionary and study for words, the bun opened its halves and embraced the cheese in an instant.

PRACTICE 5 (pages 10-11)

1.-A. Near the orchard the young pickers from Wilmont, clothed in some simple blue coveralls, had been chatting about the dance for their entire lunch break.

2.-C. Comforted, feeling tremendous relief from pressure and performance, in a mood much improved because of vacation, he started to swing his golf clubs.

3.-B. He spoke one slow, cautious sentence, like a lover who has been frequently rejected and believes that expressions of intimacy must now be guarded.

4.-D. Frenzied dancers spun near the fire just a second sooner that night, stomping loudly, their arms up, their voices whispering, their bodies writhing.

PRACTICE 6 (pages 12-14)

Note: Nonsense versions may acceptably interchange some sentence parts.

1. Bob wrote his song, rehearsed it in the evenings, sang it beautifully in the play, but the small orchestra played with the beat ahead of the singer.

2. Snaze kurped its blander, broded it with the snart, crassed it frinkly from the marton, and the plimey peesto scrunted in the tunert of a bleepert.

3. To bring work from the office is to "relax" in a state of constant worry.

4. To jeld crams near town is to murd in a zipple from a zapple.

5. A sportscaster who communicates with fans and sports' top athletes is the choice announcer who communicates with great enthusiasm and with solid knowledge.

6. The blends which croak from selfhoose and their brained nabort are the best blends which croak near thirty bleeps and near forty bloops.

7. The wrinkled skin, very dry, yet with a softness about it as appealing as the sparkle in Grandma's eyes, shone in the candlelight.

8.   An oversized saltert, quite pritert, and of a color on it as lumrious as a klanion in its woostem, plazoned from a yambrod.

PRACTICE 7 (page 15)

As if in the superhuman energy of his utterance there had been found the potency of a spell, the huge antique panels to which the speaker pointed threw slowly back, upon the instant, their ponderous and ebony jaws. It was the work of the rushing gust—but then without those doors there *did* stand the lofty and enshrouded figure of the Lady Madeline of Usher. There was blood upon her white robes, and the evidence of some bitter struggle upon every portion of her emaciated frame. For a moment she remained trembling and reeling to and fro upon the threshold—then, with a low, moaning cry, fell heavily inward upon the person of her brother, and in her violent and now final death-agonies, bore him to the floor a corpse, and a victim to the terrors he had anticipated.

PRACTICE 8 (pages 16-18)

1.   He ran from the place, leaving his suitcase, leaving the quirt, leaving the oak box of money.

2.   The father was respectable and tight, a mortgage financier and a stern, upright collection-plate passer and forecloser.

3.   After Buck Fanshaw's inquest, a meeting of the short-haired brotherhood was held, for nothing can be done on the Pacific coast without a public meeting and an expression of sentiment.

4.   With them, carrying a gnarled walking stick, was Elmo Goodhue Pipgrass, the littlest, oldest man I had ever seen.

5.   He bounded out of bed wearing a long flannel nightgown over long woolen underwear, a nightcap, and a leather jacket around his chest.

6.   Once upon a sunny morning a man who sat in a breakfast nook looked up from his scrambled eggs to see a white unicorn with a gold horn quietly cropping the roses in the garden.

7.   Then, out of a box on the bed, she removed the gleaming pair of patent-leather dancing pumps, grabbed my right foot, and shoved it into one of them, using her finger as a shoehorn.

8.   As a general rule, careful on-the-scene investigations disclose that most "unidentified" flying objects are quite ordinary phenomena, such as weather balloons, meteorites, satellites, and even once a man named Lewis Mandelbaum, who blew off the roof of the World Trade Center.

SENTENCE IMITATING

PRACTICE 1 (page 20)

1a. first
 b. second
2a. second
 b. first
3a. second
 b. first
4a. second
 b. first
5a. first
 b. second
6a. second
 b. first
7a. second
 b. first
8a. first
 b. second

PRACTICE 2 (pages 21-22)

1.   Different: b

Sources

 a.   Jack London, *All Gold Canyon*
 b.   Tate, "Ghost Men of Coronado"
 c.   Author

2.   Different: b

Sources

 a.   Bernard Malamud, *The Assistant*
 b.   Ernest Hemingway, *Green Hills of Africa*
 c.   Author

3.   Different: b

Sources

a. Author
b. Henry G. Felsen, "Horatio"
c. John Steinbeck, "Flight"

4. Different: c

Sources

a. Author
b. Joseph Conrad, "The Idiots"
c. William Faulkner, *Intruder in the Dust*

5. Different: b

Sources

a. Author
b. Ray Bradbury, *Fahrenheit 451*
c. Aldous Huxley, *Antic Hay*

6. Different: a

Sources

a. Ernest Hemingway, *For Whom the Bell Tolls*
b. Author
c. John Hersey, *Hiroshima*

PRACTICE 4 (page 27)

a. 4
b. 1
c. 3
d. 4
e. 2
f. 3
g. 2
h. 1

PRACTICE 6 (page 28)

Paragraph Two was written by Anne Morrow Lindbergh.

PRACTICE 7 (pages 28-30)

Paragraphs Three, Four, and Six are the imitations.

PRACTICE 9 (page 31)

1.   B
2.   B
3.   A

SENTENCE COMBINING

PRACTICE 1 (pages 37-38)

1.   The marble eyes rolled wide their rubber lids.
2.   The boy watched, his eyes bulging in the dark.
3.   One of the dogs, the best one, had disappeared.
4.   The huge eye on the right side of its anguished head glittered before me like a cauldron into which I might drop, screaming.
5.   Jumping to his feet and breaking off the tale, Doctor Parcival began to walk up and down in the office of the *Winesburg Eagle* where George Willard sat listening.
6.   This land was waterless, furred with the cacti which could store water and with the great-rooted brush which could reach deep into the earth for a little moisture and get along on very little.
7.   It glided through, brushing the overhanging twigs, and disappeared from the river like some slim and amphibious creature leaving the water for its lair in the forests.

PRACTICE 3 (pages 42-43)

1.   The country house, on this particular wintry afternoon, was most enjoyable.
2.   The sun was setting when the truck came back, and the earth was bloody in its setting light.
3.   He moves nervously and fast, but with a restraint that suggests that he is a cautious, thoughtful man.
4.   The girls stood aside, talking among themselves, looking over their shoulders at the boys, and the very small children rolled in the dust or clung to the hands of their older brothers or sisters.
5.   He took flour and oil, shaped a cake in a frying pan, and lighted the little stove that functioned on bottled gas.

6. When the cake was done, he set it on the windowsill to cool, heated some condensed milk diluted with water, and beat up the eggs into an omelette.

7. The fifth traveler, a withered old gentleman sitting next to the middle door across the aisle, napped fitfully upon his cane.

PRACTICE 4 (pages 43-48)

Paragraph One

(1) The high gray-flannel fog of winter closed off the Salinas Valley from the sky and from all the rest of the world. (2) On every side it sat like a lid on the mountains and made of the great valley a closed pot. (3) On the broad, level land floor the gang plows bit deep and left the black earth shining like metal where the shares had cut. (4) On the foothill ranches across the Salinas River, the yellow stubble fields seemed to be bathed in pale cold sunshine, but there was no sunshine in the valley now in December. (5) The thick willow scrub along the river flamed with sharp and positive yellow leaves.

Paragraph Two

(1) To have a dance, the women sit in a circle with their babies asleep on their backs and sing medicine songs in several parts with falsetto voices, clapping their hands in a sharp, staccato rhythm at counterpoint to the rhythm of their voices. (2) Behind their backs the men dance one behind the other, circling slowly around, taking very short, pounding steps which are again at counterpoint to both the rhythms of the singing and the clapping. (3) Now and then the men sing, too, in their deeper voices, and their dance rattles— rattles made from dry cocoons strung together with sinew cords and tied to their legs—add a sharp, high clatter like the sound of shaken gourds, very well timed because the men step accurately. (4) A Bushman dance is an infinitely complicated pattern of voices and rhythm, an orchestra of bodies, making music that is infinitely varied and always precise.

Paragraph Three

(1) Manuel, leaning against the barrera, watching the bull, waved his hand, and the gypsy ran out, trailing his cape. (2) The bull, in full gallop, pivoted and charged the cape, his head down, his tail rising. (3) The gypsy moved in a zigzag, and as he passed, the bull caught sight of him and abandoned the cape to charge the man. (4) The gyp sprinted and vaulted the red fence of the barrera as the bull struck it with his horns. (5) He tossed into it twice with his horns, banging into the wood blindly.

PRACTICE 5 (pages 49-52)

Paragraph One

(1) Outside, upon this lawn, stood an iron deer. (2) Further up on the green stood a tall brown Victorian house, quiet in the sunlight, all covered with scrolls and rococo, its windows made of blue and pink and yellow and green colored glass. (3) Upon the porch were hairy geraniums and an old swing which was hooked into the porch ceiling and which now swung back and forth, back and forth, in a little breeze. (4) At the summit of the house was a cupola with diamond leaded-glass windows and a dunce-cap roof!

Paragraph Two

(1) Upon the half decayed veranda of a small frame house that stood near the edge of a ravine near the town of Winesburg, Ohio, a fat little old man walked nervously up and down. (2) Across a long field that had been seeded for clover but that had produced only a dense crop of yellow mustard weeds, he could see the public highway along which went a wagon filled with berry pickers returning from the fields. (3) The berry pickers, youths and maidens, laughed and shouted boisterously. (4) A boy clad in a blue shirt leaped from the wagon and attempted to drag after him one of the maidens who screamed and protested shrilly. (5) The feet of the boy in the road kicked up a cloud of dust that floated across the face of the departing sun.

Paragraph Three

(1) Ulrich von Gradwitz found himself stretched on the ground, one arm numb beneath him and the other held almost as helplessly in a tight tangle of forked branches, while both legs were pinned beneath the fallen mass. (2) His heavy shooting boots had saved his feet from being crushed to pieces, but if his fractures were not as serious as they might have been, at least it was evident that he could not move from his present position till someone came to release him. (3) The descending twigs had slashed the skin of his face, and he had to wink away some drops of blood from his eyelashes before he could take in a general view of the disaster. (4) At his side, so near that under ordinary circumstances he could almost have touched him, lay Georg Znaeym, alive and struggling but obviously as helplessly pinioned down as himself. (5) All round them lay a thick-strewn wreckage of splintered branches and broken twigs.

PRACTICE 8 (pages 53-56)

1.   Now the sky was without a cloud, pale blue, delicate, luminous, scintillating with morning.

2. From ten to fifteen he distributed handbills for merchants, held horses, and ran confidential errands.

3. Nick looked down into clear, brown water, colored from the pebbly bottom, and watched the trout keeping themselves steady in the current with wavering fins.

4. On one side, beginning at the very lip of the pool, was a tiny meadow, a cool, resilient surface of green that extended to the base of the frowning wall.

5. In the stillness of the air every tree, every leaf, every bough, every tendril of creeper and every petal of minute blossoms seemed to have been bewitched into an immobility perfect and final.

6. Let every nation know, whether it wishes us well or ill, that we shall pay any price, bear any burden, meet any hardship, support any friend, oppose any foe to assure the survival and the success of liberty.

7. Four times a day the mill, the shrill wheeze of whose saws had become part of the habitual silence, blew its whistle for the hands to begin and leave off work, in blasts that seemed to shatter themselves against the thin air.

PRACTICE 10 (pages 57-59)

(1) Marilyn Monroe, with her legendary beauty, one of a series of blonde sex symbols before her like Jean Harlow and Betty Grable, was a rare and, in her case, tragic combination of innocent little girl and experienced woman. (2) At some times amusing to people and at other times irritating, her playfulness, her giggling, her personal and professional insecurity, her desire for protection were child-like, rooted in a fear of responsibility. (3) She suffered from a confused identity, wondering whether she was loved for herself or for her public image, an identity as sex symbol which she resented yet worked hard to create. (4) Although many people and critics damned her as a mindless woman without acting ability, just as many others praised her as an uneducated but very intelligent woman and a talented actress. (5) When she entered middle age, having married and divorced older men who she thought would be her protectors, having been institutionalized several times for psychiatric problems, using drugs to alter her moods, imagining rejection by Hollywood and the world, she felt helpless, desperate, afraid, and committed suicide, to the regret of Hollywood, to the shock of the world; and only now, unfortunately, she has become appreciated for her humanity, intelligence, talent, and, of course, for her beauty.

SENTENCE EXPANDING

PRACTICE 4 (page 69)

1. In the hall stood an enormous trunk, **behind the ladder that led to the roof, just opposite Hedger's door.**

2.   All members of the staff, **from the ornithologists and researchers to the girls in the bookstore, wore plastic tags bearing their names and color photographs.**

3.   Jerry stood on the landing, **smiling nervously.**

4.   They lived in a square two-flat house tightly packed among identical houses on a fog-enveloped street in the Sunset district of San Francisco, **less than a mile from the ocean, more than three miles from Nob Hill, more than three thousand miles from Times Square.**

5.   His teeth, **while strong and sharp,** were, **as weapons of offense,** pitifully inadequate by comparison with the mighty fighting fangs of the anthropoids.

6.   **In the long, burning, murmurous Virginia summers,** he used to ride, alone, **back into the country towards the mountains, along the clay roads, dusty and red, and through the sweet-scented long grasses of the fields.**

7.   **With an exclamation** she tossed her book to the deck, **where it sprawled at a straddle,** and hurried to the rail.

8.   **When one half of the world is angry at the other half, or one half of a nation is angry at the rest, or one side of town feuds with the other side,** it is hardly surprising, **when you stop to think about it,** that so many people lose their tempers with so many other people.

PRACTICE 7 (pages 71-72)

1.   She sprang dynamically to her feet, **clinching her hands,** then swiftly and noiselessly crossed over to her bed and, **from underneath it,** dragged out her suitcase.

2.   He stood there, **rubbing his injured shoulder,** and Rainsford, **with fear again gripping his heart,** heard the general's mocking laugh ring through the jungle.

3.   **Five, six, eight times** he knocked the big man down, and the big man came again, **staggering, slavering, raving, vainly trying to rend and smash.**

4.   We spent several evenings together, and the last one was the funniest, **because this time Joyce, who always had quite a lot to drink, got really potted.**

5.   That night in the south upstairs chamber, **a hot little room where a full-leafed chinaberry tree shut all the air from the single window,** Emmett lay in a kind of trance.

6.   **With something of the childish belief in miracles with which he had so often gone to class, all his lessons unlearned,** Paul dressed and dashed whistling down the corridor to the elevator.

7.   Adolph Knipe took a sip of stout, **testing the malty-bitter flavor, feeling the trickle of cold liquid as it traveled down his throat and settled in the top**

of his stomach, cool at first, then spreading and becoming warm, making a little area of warmness inside him.

PRACTICE 8 (pages 72-73)

1.   On the outskirts of town, **she came upon her destination,** though at first she did not realize it.

2.   **He stirred and drank it down,** sweet, hot, and warming in his empty stomach.

3.   When the hostess saw that I was awake and that my safety belt was already fastened, **she smiled efficiently and moved on down the aisle,** waking the other passengers and asking them to fasten their safety belts.

4.   Running up the street with all his might, **Marty could see that the game would start any minute now.**

5.   Placing a cigarette between his lips, **he struck a match, inhaled the smoke hurriedly and put out the light.**

6.   At night, untired after the day's work, **he washed first in turpentine and then in water, and talked with the family.**

7.   There, in a four-roomed, lime-washed, thatched cottage, **Shawn made his life, and, though his friends hinted his needs and obligations, no thought came to him of bringing a wife into the place.**

PRACTICE 12 (pages 75-76)

1.   The chest was there, **locked and heavy.**

2.   **Standing in an aisle in a library,** he can feel the eyes on him.

3.   She made the best meatloaf in the world, **and would give it to me raw, seasoned with onions and green peppers, from the bowl.**

4.   **Now, lying in the ditch with Billy and the scouts after having been shot at,** Weary made Billy take a very close look at his trench knife.

5.   **In the monastery where they stayed, Parador de San Francisco,** the gardens were laid out so neatly, **with fountains and stone benches, and stones inlaid on the walkways.**

6.   **Above the open shirt** a pale silk scarf is tied around his neck, **almost completely hiding from view the throat whose creases are the only sign of his age.**

7.   **After this climax,** the four animals continued to lead their lives, **so rudely broken in upon by civil war, in great joy and contentment, undisturbed by further risings or invasions.**

8.   He went into the kitchen, **where the moonlight called his attention to a half bottle of champagne on the kitchen table, all that was left from the reception in the tent.**

PRACTICE 13 (page 77)

The mouth widened gapingly **as the lips drew back and drew back, meeting the nose and disappearing in an oral ring of jutting teeth.** The fingernails went black and peeled off, and then there were only bones, **still dressed with rings, clicking and clenching like castanets.** Dust puffed through the fibers of the linen shirt. The bald and wrinkled head became a skull. The pants, **with nothing to fill them out,** fell away to broomsticks clad in black silk.

PARAGRAPH EXPANDING

PRACTICE 2 (pages 85-86)

1. The admiral was now faced with a decision no man should have to make. **If the wingman stayed on, he would surely run out of fuel and lose his own plane and probably his life as well.** But to command him to leave a downed companion was inhuman and any pilot aboard the Savo would prefer to risk his own life and his plane rather than to leave a man adrift in the freezing sea before the helicopter had spotted him.

2. Laughter blew across the moon-colored lawn from the house of Clarisse **and her father and mother and the uncle who smiled so quietly and so earnestly. Above all, their laughter was relaxed and hearty and not forced in any way, coming from the house that was so brightly lit this late at night while all the other houses were kept to themselves in darkness.** Montag heard the voices talking, talking, talking, giving, talking, weaving, reweaving their hypnotic web.

3. At times, feeling the wind on my brow, I went numb with horror. In my imagination I saw armies of ants and cockroaches calling to one another and scurrying toward my head, to some place under the top of my skull, where they would build new nests. **There they would eat out my thoughts, one after another, until I would become as empty as the shell of a pumpkin from which all the fruit has been scraped out.**

4. He woke just after two and heard the wind. **It wasn't the storm and bluster of a south-westerly gale, bringing rain. It was the east wind, cold and dry.**

5. They sat down by the fire again. **Outside, the wind was higher than ever, and the old man jumped nervously at the sound of a door banging upstairs.** A silence, unusual and depressing, settled upon all three, which lasted until the old couple arose to retire for the night.

6. **Six days after he arrived in town his animal was struck by the Tulare Street trolley and seriously injured.** The following day the animal passed away, most likely of internal injuries, on the corner of Mariposa and Fulton

streets. **The animal sank to the pavement, fell on the Indian's leg, groaned, and died.**

7. **Mrs. Sharp screamed.** All eyes turned to look down the street where a figure had suddenly materialized in the darkness, and the sound of measured footsteps on concrete grew louder and louder as it walked toward them. **Sally Bishop let out a stifled cry and grabbed Tommy's shoulder.**

PRACTICE 3 (pages 86-88)

1. c, b, a
2. c, a, b
3. c, a, b
4. d, b, a, c

PRACTICE 4 (pages 88-90)

1. b, c, a
2. a, c, b
3. b, a, c
4. a, c, d, b
5. c, b, e, a, d
6. b, f, e, d, a, c
7. d, b, c, e, g, a, h, f

PRACTICE 5 (pages 90-93)

A. b
B. c
C. c
D. a
E. c

PRACTICE 6 (pages 93-94)

A. 3
B. 1
C. 4
D. 5
E. 2

PRACTICE 7 (pages 94-95)

From Ray Bradbury, *The Martian Chronicles:* Original Sequence: 5, 11, 14, 10, 2, 7

The rocket landed on a lawn of green grass. Outside, upon this lawn, stood an iron deer. Further up on the green stood a tall brown Victorian house, quiet in the sunlight, all covered with scrolls and rococo, its windows made of blue and pink and yellow and green colored glass. Upon the porch were hairy geraniums and an old swing which was hooked into the porch ceiling and which now swung back and forth, back and forth, in a little breeze. At the summit of the house was a cupola with diamond leaded-glass windows and a dunce-cap roof! Through the front window you could see a piece of music titled "Beautiful Ohio" sitting on the music rest.

From Harper Lee, *To Kill a Mockingbird:* Original Sequence: 13, 6, 12, 1

I looked from his hands to his sand-stained khaki pants; my eyes traveled up his thin frame to his torn denim shirt. His face was as white as his hands, but for a shadow on his jutting chin. His cheeks were thin to hollowness; his mouth was wide; there were shallow, almost delicate indentations at his temples, and his gray eyes were so colorless I thought he was blind. His hair was dead and thin, almost feathery on top of his head.

From Edgar Allan Poe, "The Cask of Amontillado": Original Sequence: 9, 15, 3, 16, 4, 8

At the most remote end of the crypt there appeared another less spacious. Its walls had been lined with human remains piled to the vault overhead, in the fashion of the great catacombs of Paris. Three sides of this interior crypt were still ornamented in this manner. From the fourth the bones had been thrown down, and lay promiscuously upon the earth, forming at one point a mound of some size. Within the wall thus exposed by the displacing of the bones, we perceived a still interior recess, in depth about four feet, in width three, in height six or seven. It seemed to have been constructed for no especial use within itself, but formed merely the interval between two of the colossal supports of the roof of the catacombs, and was backed by one of their circumscribing walls of solid granite.

PRACTICE 8 (pages 98-99)

A.   1. Every morning, after Jody had curried and brushed the pony, he let down the barrier of the stall, and Gabilan thrust past him and raced down the barn and into the corral. 2. **Around and around he galloped, and sometimes he jumped forward and landed on stiff legs.** 3. **He stood quivering, stiff ears forward, eyes rolling so that the whites showed, pretending to be frightened.**

4. At last he walked snorting to the water-trough and buried his nose in the water up to the nostrils. 5. Jody was proud then, for he knew that was the way to judge a horse. 6. Poor horses only touched their lips to the water, but a fine spirited beast put his whole nose and mouth under, and only left room to breathe.

B.   1. Scarlett O'Hara was not beautiful, but men seldom realized it when caught by her charm as the Tarleton twins were. 2. In her face were too sharply blended the delicate features of her mother, a Coast aristocrat of French descent, and the heavy ones of her florid Irish father. 3. But it was an arresting face, pointed of chin, square of jaw. 4. **Her eyes were pale green without a touch of hazel, starred with bristly black lashes and slightly tilted at the ends. 5. Above them, her thick black brows slanted upward, cutting a startling oblique line in her magnolia-white skin—that skin so prized by Southern women and so carefully guarded with bonnets, veils and mittens against hot Georgia suns.**

C.   1. But winter was full half the year. 2. **The snow began at Thanksgiving and fell snow upon snow till Fast Day, thawing between the storms, and packing harder and harder against the break-up in the spring, when it covered the ground in solid levels three feet high, and lay heaped in drifts, that defied the sun far into May.** 3. When it did not snow, the weather was keenly clear, and commonly very still. 4. **Then the landscape at noon had a stereoscopic glister under the high sun that burned in a heaven without a cloud, and at setting stained the sky and the white waste with freezing pink and violet.** 5. On such days the farmers and lumbermen came in to the village stores, and made a stiff and feeble stir about their doorways, and the school children gave the street a little life and color, as they went to and from the Academy in their red and blue woolens.

D.   1. The pass was high and wide and he jumped for it, feeling it slap flatly against his hands, as he shook his hips to throw off the halfback who was diving at him. 2. The center floated by, his hands desperately brushing Darling's knee as Darling picked his feet up high and delicately ran over a blocker and an opposing linesman in a jumble on the ground near the scrimmage line. 3. **He had ten yards in the clear and picked up speed, breathing easily, feeling his thigh pads rising and falling against his legs, listening to the sound of cleats behind him, pulling away from them, watching the other backs heading him off toward the sideline, the whole picture, the men closing in on him, the blockers fighting for position, the ground he had to cross, all suddenly clear in his head, for the first time in his life not a meaningless confusion of men, sounds, speed.** 4. He smiled a little to himself as he ran, holding the ball lightly in front of him with his two hands, his knees pumping high, his hips twisting in the almost girlish run of a back in a broken field. 5. **The first halfback came at him and he fed him his leg, then swung at the last moment, took**

the shock of the man's shoulder without breaking stride, ran right through him, his cleats biting securely into the turf. 6. There was only the safety man now, coming warily at him, his arms crooked, hands spread. 7. **Darling tucked the ball in, spurted at him, driving hard, hurling himself along, his legs pounding, knees high, all two hundred pounds bunched into controlled attack.** 8. He was sure he was going to get past the safety man. 9. **Without thought, his arms and legs working beautifully together, he headed right for the safety man, stiff-armed him, feeling blood spurt instantaneously from the man's nose onto his hand, seeing his face go awry, head turned, mouth pulled to one side.** 10. He pivoted away, keeping the arm locked, dropping the safety man as he ran easily toward the goal line, with the drumming of cleats diminishing behind him.

PRACTICE 9 (pages 102-103)

Description of a Delicatessen

A.   . . . Down in the town on a corner of what was, comparatively speaking, our busiest street, there was a neat and attractively stocked delicatessen store, a branch, if I am not mistaken, of a Wiesbaden firm. It was patronized by the best society. My way to school led me past this shop daily and I had stopped in many times, coin in hand, to buy cheap candies, fruit drops or barley sugar. But on going in one day I found it empty not only of customers but of attendants as well. There was a little bell on a spring over the door, and this had rung as I entered; but either the inner room was empty or its occupants had not heard the bell—I was and remained alone. The glass door at the rear was covered by some pleated material. At first the emptiness surprised and startled me; it even gave me an uncanny feeling; but presently I began to look about me, for never before had I been able to contemplate undisturbed the delights of such a spot. It was a narrow room, with a rather high ceiling, and crowded from floor to ceiling with goodies. 1. **There were rows and rows of hams and sausages of all shapes and colours—white, yellow, red, and black; fat and lean and round and long—rows of canned preserves, cocoa and tea, bright translucent glass bottles of honey, marmalade, and jam; round bottles and slender bottles, filled with liqueurs and punch—all these things crowded every inch of the shelves from top to bottom.** 2. **Then there were glass showcases where smoked mackerel, lampreys, flounders, and eels were displayed on platters to tempt the appetite.** 3. **There were dishes of Italian salad, crayfish spreading their claws on blocks of ice, sprats pressed flat and gleaming goldenly from open boxes; choice fruits—garden strawberries and grapes as beautiful as though they had come from the Promised Land; rows of sardine tins and those fascinating little white earthenware jars of caviar and "foie gras."** 4. **Plump chickens dangled their necks from the top shelf, and** there were trays of cooked meats, ham, tongue, beef, and veal, smoked salmon and breast of goose, with the slender slicing knife lying ready at hand. 5. There were all sorts of cheeses under glass bells, brick-red, milk-white, and marbled, also the creamy ones that overflow their silver foil in golden waves. 6. Artichokes, bundles of asparagus, truffles, little live sausages in silver paper—all these things lay heaped in rich profusion; while on other tables stood open tin boxes full of fine biscuits, spice cakes piled in criss-cross layers, and glass urns full of dessert candies and candied fruits.

Description of Market Sheds

A.   Today, under the long skylit roofs of the market sheds, the long trestle tables are spread with miles of food. 1. There is meat on the meat stalls now—carabao, pork, and beef in long, red, gluteal rivers—and entrails, organs and tripe in slithering mounds. 2. There are great mountains of cabbages, greens, beans, cucumbers, lettuce, white radishes, leeks and squash, and of breadfruit, pineapple, mango, lansone, guava, blimbing, and durian in semiquarantine and smelling like cheese. 3. One entire row of tables and stalls deals in nothing but blazing bananas, golden fingers clutched in clumps and clusters, yellow masses piled high, great green claws hanging down, and golden crowns swirling like blazing haloes as they hang on strings and the air is alive with the gold of bananas and the smell of their heady ferment.

B.   But more important than anything else, for it is the manna of the Philippines, there are fish in the fishmarket. 1. I walk between hills of scales down aisles of opalescent sheen, and see fish with flattened gills shimmering and slithering, smelling of salt and sea and covered with slime; fish of every color, shape and feel, soft, hard, red, yellow, black, blue, purple, jade, and green. 2. Here are Crustacea like round ribbon rosettes, like flowers just opening, like pools in surf-drenched rock; crab, crayfish, mussels, oysters, and clams. 3. There are octopuses like wet black rubber tubing, and like dark purple bruises. 4. There are fish like whales and fish like midgets, like balls and those like swords, fish wide and flat, tall and thin, round and star-shaped, spiked and spindly, and fishes not at all like fishes. 5. All these are fresh, but their like may be found shriveled, dried, salted, cured and stinking high and loud, in all sizes, from minnow-size bait in countless hordes to huge crosscuts of whale-like tunas and dried octopus hanging from strings overhead.

PRACTICE 10 (pages 104-106)

Starting Sentences

1.   At nearly midnight, the night before the bomb was dropped, an announcer on the city's radio station said that about two hundred B-29s were

approaching southern Honshu and advised the population of Hiroshima to evacuate to their designated "safe areas." Mrs. Hatsuyo Nakamura, the tailor's widow, who lived in the section called Noboricho and who had long had a habit of doing as she was told, got her three children—a ten-year-old boy, Toshio, an eight-year-old girl, Yaeko, and a five-year-old girl, Myeko—out of bed and dressed them and walked with them to the military area known as the East Parade Ground, on the northeast edge of the city. There she unrolled some mats and the children lay down on them. They slept until about two, when they were awakened by the roar of the planes going over Hiroshima.

2.   **Down on the beach a match flared, and in its momentary light Kino saw that two of the men were sleeping, curled up like dogs, while the third watched, and he saw the glint of the rifle in the match light.** And then the match died, but it left a picture on Kino's eyes. He could see it, just how each man was, two sleeping curled and the third squatting in the sand with the rifle between his knees.

3.   **The Radley Place had ceased to terrify me, but it was no less gloomy, no less chilly under its great oaks, and no less uninviting.** Mr. Nathan Radley could still be seen on a clear day, walking to and from town; we knew Boo was there, for the same old reason—nobody'd seen him carried out yet. I sometimes felt a twinge of remorse, when passing by the old place, at ever having taken part in what must have been sheer torment to Arthur Radley—what reasonable recluse wants children peeping through his shutters, delivering greetings on the end of a fishing-pole, wandering in his collards at night?

4.   **The concussion knocked the air across and down the river, turned the men over like dominos in a line, blew the water in lifting sprays, and blew the dust and made the trees above them mourn with a great wind passing away south.** Montag crushed himself down, squeezing himself small, eyes tight. He blinked once. And in that instant saw the city, instead of the bombs, in the air. They had displaced each other. For another of those impossible instants the city stood, rebuilt and unrecognizable, taller than it had ever hoped or strived to be, taller than man had built it, erected at last in gouts of shattered concrete and sparkles of torn metal into a mural hung like a reversed avalanche, a million colors, a million oddities, a door where a window should be, a top for a bottom, a side for a back, and then the city rolled over and fell down dead.

5.   **While I was waiting around for Phoebe in the museum, right inside the doors and all, these two little kids came up to me and asked me if I knew where the mummies were.** The one little kid, the one that asked me, had his pants open. I told him about it. So he buttoned them up right where he was standing talking to me—he didn't even bother to go behind a post or anything. He killed me. I would've laughed, but I was afraid I'd feel like vomiting again, so I didn't. "Where're the mummies, fella?" the kid said again. "Ya know?"

6. **Then Jody stood and watched the pony, and he saw things he had never noticed about any other horse, the sleek, sliding flank muscles and the cords of the buttocks, which flexed like a closing fist, and the shine the sun put on the red coat.** Having seen horses all his life, Jody had never looked at them very closely before. But now he noticed the moving ears which gave expression and even inflection of expression to the face. The pony talked with his ears. You could tell exactly how he felt about everything by the way his ears pointed. Sometimes they were stiff and upright and sometimes lax and sagging. They went back when he was angry or fearful, and forward when he was anxious and curious and pleased; and their exact position indicated which emotion he had.

7. **She made breakfast and, when Guy had gone, did the sinkful of dishes and put the kitchen to rights.** She opened windows in the living room and bedroom—the smell of last night's fire still lingered in the apartment—made the bed, and took a shower; a long one, first hot and then cold. She stood capless and immobile under the downpour, waiting for her head to clear and her thoughts to find an order and conclusion.

8. **The motorcycle on the sidewalk speeded up and skidded obliquely into a plate-glass window, the front wheel bucking and climbing the brick base beneath the window.** A single large section of glass slipped edge-down to the sidewalk and fell slowly toward the cyclist who, with his feet spread and kicking at the cement, backed clumsily away from it. Bleeker could feel the crash in his teeth.

Middle Sentences

9. He was panic-stricken. **He ran furiously to and fro, dodging when there was no need to dodge, and in his anxiety to see on every side of him at once, stumbling.** For a moment he was down and they heard his fall. Far away in the circumferential wall a little doorway looked like heaven, and he set off in a wild rush for it. He did not look round at his pursuers until it was gained, and he had stumbled across the bridge, clambered a little way among the rocks, to the surprise and dismay of a young llama, who went leaping out of sight, and lay down sobbing for breath.

10. The only doctor's office I was familiar with was Dr. Hapgood's, where Mother used to take us every year just before school opened for our annual checkup. **His waiting room was big and musty and smelled of crayon wax almost as strongly as it smelled of the rubbing alcohol he used to clean the place where he was going to give us a shot.** The boxes of crayons stood on the magazine rack along with various coloring books, and Grace and I forgot our fears by fighting over the least worn-down crayons and the prettiest coloring book until it was our turn to be led into the inner sanctum where heaven knew what might await us. There were no crayons or coloring books in Dr.

Harvey's waiting room, but I'm sure if there had been I would, out of habit and nervousness, have pounced on them.

11.   Felicidad was terribly excited and nervous as they went to meet the two boys in the lobby of the dance hall, *El Palacio.* The fight with her mother had not been resolved, and she had taken matters into her own hands, but none the less, she was more frightened than she wanted Carmen to know. She had asked her all about the boy who would be her escort. She knew his name was David Krusky and that he worked with Ramon as a shipping clerk in some big warehouse. **According to Carmen, he wasn't really handsome, but he was nice-looking and a lot of fun.** Aside from Jim next door, who came and talked with her often when she did babysitting for Mrs. Benton, David would be the first New York boy she had met, and this would certainly be her first date.

12.   He was the smartest boy in the Muskogee County School—for colored children. Everybody even remotely connected with the school knew this. **The teacher always pronounced his name with profound gusto as she pointed him out as the ideal student.** Once I heard her say: "If he were white he might, some day, become President." Only Aaron Crawford wasn't white; quite the contrary. His skin was so solid black that it glowed, reflecting an inner virtue that was strange, and beyond my comprehension.

13.   I had hoped that the white moderate would understand that law and order exist for the purpose of establishing justice and that when they fail in this purpose they become the dangerously structured dams that block the flow of social progress. **I had hoped that the white moderate would understand that the present tension in the South is a necessary phase of the transition from an obnoxious negative peace, in which the Negro passively accepted his unjust plight, to a substantive and positive peace, in which all men will respect the dignity and worth of human personality.** Actually, we who engage in nonviolent direct action are not the creators of tension. We merely bring to the surface the hidden tension that is already alive. We bring it out in the open, where it can be seen and dealt with. Like a boil that can never be cured so long as it is covered up but must be opened with all its ugliness to the natural medicines of air and light, injustice must be exposed, with all the tension its exposure creates, to the light of human conscience and the air of national opinion before it can be cured.

14.   He knelt down and found the tuna under the stern with the gaff and drew it toward him keeping it clear of the coiled lines. **Holding the line with his left shoulder again, and bracing on his left hand and arm, he took the tuna off the gaff hook and put the gaff back in place.** He put one knee on the fish and cut strips of dark red meat longitudinally from the back of the head to the tail. They were wedge-shaped strips and he cut them from next to the back bone down to the edge of the belly. When he had cut six strips he spread them out on the wood of the bow, wiped his knife on his trousers, and lifted the carcass of the bonito by the tail and dropped it overboard.

15. Dr. Jeffers was waiting for David Leiber the day he came to take his wife and new child home. **He motioned Leiber to a chair in his office, gave him a cigar, lit one for himself, sat on the edge of his desk, puffing solemnly for a long moment.** Then he cleared his throat, looked David Leiber straight on and said, "Your wife doesn't like her child, Dave."

16. She shot him. **The heavy slug struck him in the shoulder and flattened and tore out a piece of his shoulderblade.** The flash and roar smothered him, and he staggered back and fell to the floor. She moved slowly toward him, cautiously, as she might toward a wounded animal. He stared up into her eyes, which inspected him impersonally. She tossed the pistol on the floor beside him and walked out of the house.

Ending Sentences

17. The turret opened. A man's head and shoulders appeared, looking toward the sniper. The sniper raised his rifle and fired. The head fell heavily on the turret wall. The woman darted toward the side street. The sniper fired again. **The woman whirled round and fell with a shriek into the gutter.**

18. The policeman on the beat moved up the avenue impressively. The impressiveness was habitual and not for show, for spectators were few. **The time was barely ten o'clock at night, but chilly gusts of wind with a taste of rain in them had well nigh depeopled the street.**

19. He could see now that what the new kid was eating was a slice of rye bread covered with apple sauce. He could see, too, that the new kid was smaller than he was, and had a narrow face and a large nose with a few little freckles across the bridge. **He was wearing Boy Scout pants and a brown woolen pullover, and on the back of his head was a skullcap made from the crown of a man's felt hat, the edge turned up and cut into sharp points that were ornamented with brass paper clips.**

20. The gypsy was walking out toward the bull again, walking heel-and-toe, insultingly, like a ballroom dancer, the red shafts of the banderillos twitching with his walk. **The bull watched him, not fixed now, hunting him, but waiting to get close enough so he could be sure of getting him, getting the horns into him.**

21. She had a white nape to her neck and short red hair above it, and Shawn liked the color and wave of that flame. And he liked the set of her shoulders and the way the white neck had of leaning a little forward as she sat at her prayers—or her dreams. And the service over, Shawn used to stay in his seat so that he might get one quick but sure look at her face as she passed out. And he liked her face, too—the wide-set gray eyes, cheekbones firmly curved, clean-molded lips, austere yet sensitive. **And he smiled pityingly at himself that one of her name should make his pulses stir—for she was an O'Grady.**

22.   Outside, his carpetbag in his hand, he stood for a time in the barnyard. He could see that it was still early, a moonlit summer night, cooling off now so that the river mists were flowing up into the draws. **He could hear the soft, slow movements of the animals in their stalls and once in awhile, as the air freshened, a slight fluttering of leaves.**

23.   He lifted the knocker, and it creaked up stiffly, as if it had never before been used. He let it fall, and it startled him with its booming loudness. He thought he heard steps within; the door remained closed. Again Rainsford lifted the heavy knocker, and let it fall. The door opened then, opened as suddenly as if it were on a spring, and Rainsford stood blinking in the river of glaring gold light that poured out. The first thing Rainsford's eyes discerned was the largest man Rainsford had ever seen—a gigantic creature, solidly made and black-bearded to the waist. **In his hand the man held a long-barreled revolver, and he was pointing it straight at Rainsford's heart.**

24.   Only a few yards off, a tall, lean stranger approached, stooping slightly and bearing close to his dark coat, a white parcel, high, as though he meant to proffer it to the two boys before him. An instant David stared, and suddenly in the space of one stride, it was neither stranger nor parcel he saw, but his own father, and the right hand against his coat was hanging from a sling and swathed in bandages. **He screamed.**